Laker

Portrait of a Legend

Laker

Portrait of a Legend

Don Mosey

Macdonald
Queen Anne Press

A Queen Anne Press BOOK

© Don Mosey 1989

First published in Great Britain in 1989 by
Queen Anne Press, a division of
Macdonald & Co (Publishers) Ltd
66–73 Shoe Lane
London
EC4P 4AB

A member of Maxwell Pergamon Publishing Corporation plc

Design – Judith Clarke

Jacket photographs – Front: Jim Laker *Keystone*
                 Back: Old Trafford, 1956 *Sport & General*

British Library Cataloguing in Publication Data

Mosey, Don, *1924–*
  Jim Laker
  1. Cricket. Laker, Jim, 1922–1986
  I. Title
  796.35'8'0924

  ISBN 0–356–17162–0

Typeset by Butler & Tanner Limited, Frome, Somerset
Printed and bound in Great Britain by
Hazell Watson & Viney Limited
Aylesbury, Bucks

Acknowledgements

My warmest thanks are due to Mrs Lilly Laker for her help and co-operation and to Jim's many friends and admirers who have contributed to this book

CONTENTS

INTRODUCTION

In the quarter of a century since Jim Laker last bowled a ball in first-class cricket, a whole generation has grown up thinking of the burly man with a homely Yorkshire accent and a dry sense of humour simply as a television commentator. Cricket being a game deeply involved with history and statistics, most of them will be at least aware that, like all his colleagues in the television commentary team, he was a player at one time. However such was the chequered nature of Laker's career, many of the present generation will, inevitably, be unaware of just how good he was.

The extent of his ability is obscured to a large extent by statistics, especially when one compares the number of Test Matches played today with their relative paucity 25 and 30 years ago. Laker was, in the eyes of those who played with and against him, without argument the best off-break bowler in a world which had rather a lot of them and yet he played in fewer than half the Tests which took place during his first-class career. Today, any sort of accomplished off-spinner is a rarity, as the art of spin bowling of all kinds – with a few notable exceptions – continues to die a slow and tragic death. If Laker had played 25 to 30 years later than he did he would have been an automatic choice for his country and would have undoubtedly taken part in more than 100 international games. Just how many wickets he would have gathered is a matter for conjecture, but on a purely *pro rata* basis he would now almost certainly have become the leading wicket-taker in the world at Test level.

In many ways Jim Laker's career was one of contrasts and con-tradictions: he was quite simply the best, but that fact – inexplicably – was very often ignored by the selectors of his day. He was an unde-monstrative cricketer, almost to the point of self-effacement, but he held strong views on the way the game should be played and administered; when he aired those views publicly in an era in which professional cricketers were expected to keep their opinions to themselves he created a major sensation. He was, and remained to the end of his days, unrepentant at having stirred up a hornets' nest in 1960 by publishing a book which was openly and trenchantly critical of the establishment.

He believed passionately that he and his fellow craftsmen were worthy of better treatment than they received and his beliefs were reflected in that first book, *Over to Me*, which brought him into direct conflict with both the MCC and his county, Surrey. Yet in his political thinking he was the very opposite of a radical.

He was a Yorkshireman who thought in almost every way like a man from the broad acres and yet he devoted himself to his adopted county both as a player and, later, as an administrator.

He overcame a natural shyness to become an accomplished speaker and, while publicly proclaiming that in this and other contexts the labourer was worthy of his hire, he nevertheless did a tremendous amount of speaking without any fee at all if he felt the cause was a worthy one.

He was a shrewd man with an acute business brain; he trained as a banker and he dabbled in a number of business enterprises at any one of which he might have gone on to achieve great success, but in the end it was as a communicator that he made his mark. As a television commentator he earned the greatest respect within the game for his intelligent assessments while irritating many listeners with the style of his delivery.

He was a man's man in public, a devoted husband, father and grand-father in private; only those who knew him really well were able to observe this particular contrast in detail.

He was accused by some contemporaries of a lack of determination – that he was reluctant to bowl when conditions were against him. He resented one such accusation from Peter May strongly enough to refuse to tour under him – and yet the following pages are full of tributes from observers who attest to his courage and indeed the versatility of his bowling in unhelpful circumstances.

There are so many contradictions – both personal and professional – in the story of Jim Laker that it is indeed a tangled web that has to be unravelled. What no one could ever doubt, however, was his true greatness as a bowler of off-breaks, an art he fashioned himself without expert tuition or guidance but with a characteristic determination in the pursuit of excellence which reached its peak in the year 1956 ...

OLD TRAFFORD, 1956

On the morning of 16 May, 1956, Jim Laker arrived at The Oval feeling more than a little jaded. Both his young daughters had been ill during the night and father had done his share of ministering to them. He would have been happy to see Stuart Surridge, the Surrey captain, come back from tossing the coin with Ian Johnson, skipper of the touring Australians, to announce that the bowlers could put their feet up for the day – but such things rarely work out when they're wanted and this time was no exception. Surrey took the field and with the Bedser twins absent the remaining bowlers were expecting a reasonable amount of hard labour. Laker was given the ball at 12.20 p.m. and he retained it until the tourists were all out, 40 minutes from the end of the day, when his figures were 46–18–88–10.

Out came the record books to reveal that the only other Englishman to have taken all 10 Australian wickets was Edward Barratt, also of Surrey (though born in County Durham), 78 years previously. Many people have claimed they saw this new piece of history written but the truth is that relatively few can actually have done so because contemporary reports speak of only a small crowd present on the first morning of the game and the first wicket (Jim Burke, lbw) fell before lunch. Without such legendary figures as Bradman, Hassett and Morris, the Australians were not quite the attraction they had proved on their two previous post-war visits and indeed they had not looked a particularly exciting side in their three earlier matches. That is not to say, however, that they were expected to be an easy side to beat; any Australian side still represented the ultimate test for England, notwithstanding the shocks administered by the West Indies in 1950.

Surridge might have taken the new ball just before 4 p.m. on the first afternoon and Jim himself later recalled that during the tea interval he gently suggested to his captain that after 30 consecutive overs he might be about due for a rest. But Stuart Surridge, a remarkably intuitive skipper, already sensed that they were on the threshold of something quite remarkable. 'It was', Surridge recalls, 'the most wonderful piece of spin bowling I have ever seen.' And at that time Laker had taken the only four wickets to fall. It is too much to believe that Surridge could have anticipated an all-10 performance, but if he merely saw in the off-spinner his best means of dismissing the Australians relatively cheaply, who is to say that he was wrong in calling for one more effort from his one successful bowler after the second interval? That apart, it was the beginning of Jim's benefit year and a bit of window-dressing could well have been helpful, to say the least.

So he toiled on and when he had nine wickets in the bag that great all-rounder Keith Miller (who had gone in at number five) was joined by one John William Wilson, a Victorian slow left-armer who was destined to make no great impact on Test cricket. In fact how many cricket enthusiasts can honestly say they remember the name? Clearly, there was now a conscious effort on the part of other bowlers to give Laker the chance to take all 10 and Keith Miller was not a man to let such an opportunity slip by. He launched a colourful attack on Tony Lock, at the other end, while farming the bowling to keep Wilson away from Laker as the score climbed from 217 for nine to 259. In 25 minutes, Jim had no chance to have a go at Wilson, and then, off the fifth ball of his 46th over, he saw Miller take a single. The last ball was enough to remove Wilson, caught at the wicket by Roy Swetman and Laker had taken all 10 for 88.

In the *Daily Telegraph*, E. W. Swanton reported:

> J. Laker performed a great feat of bowling at The Oval yesterday. The adjective in these days is, surely, persistently misused. But nothing less describes the unfailing accuracy, the power of spin, and the little variations played on the theme of perfect length which brought him the glory, all but unparalleled, of taking 10 Australian wickets in an innings.

While not many people can have seen the first wicket fall, considerably more saw the last one go down, because while the crowd increased during the afternoon in the natural order of things, many people raced to The Oval in the later stages of the Australian innings as word went round that history was possibly being made in Kennington. In the *Daily Mail*, Alex Bannister described how the crowd, 'whose excitement had been raised to fever-pitch as wicket after wicket fell to the same bowler, cheered Laker to the pavilion'. And they stayed to cheer again when the ball he had used was presented to Laker by the Surrey president, Marshal of the Royal Air Force, Lord Tedder. An astonishing season was under way.

Jim was a keen betting man, particularly on horses, and in later years he enjoyed quietly musing on the odds he might have been offered against taking all 10 wickets of the Australian touring team *twice* in one season. I have tried the same ploy myself on Godfrey Evans, Jim's wicketkeeping contemporary for England, who subsequently became advisor and public relations man for Ladbrokes when they were allowed to place betting-tents on first-class cricket grounds. The answer is, inevitably, wordless – a roll of the eyes, a snort, a wave of the arms, but no price. The odds, in fact, would be incalculable. No one, no matter how fertile his imagination, how burning his ambition, how iron-clad his confidence, could possibly visualise such a double. But Jim Laker did it. On the following page the match scorecard is reproduced in full.

Before we leave The Oval, 1956, it should be recorded that Laker scored 43 with the bat including two fours and a six in one over from Ian Johnson, the Aussies' off-spinner, and then watched with great pleasure as his partner, Tony Lock, took seven second-innings wickets for 49. Surrey, county champions for the previous four years and destined to remain so that year and for the next two, had become the first county to beat an Australian touring side since 1912 – and that had been a poor team ravaged by injuries and illness.

In a way which has become commonplace in the eighties but which was almost unheard of in the fifties, Jim Laker was now the darling of the media. The *News Chronicle* signed him up for, first, a potted biography and then a series of instructional articles illustrated by close-up pictures of his grip on the ball. The manufacturers of the nutritional drink, Lucozade, announced: 'Jim Laker takes 10 wickets for 88 runs. How's that for sustained energy?' And their advertisement went on to proclaim that the Laker family replaced lost energy by drinking the stuff. Jim was pictured nursing the three-year-old Fiona and 20-months-old Angela, romping with them, putting them to bed; and his wife Lilly, despite a natural diffidence at being involved, got into the picture too, kissing her husband farewell as she took the girls off for a holiday; cartoonists depicted Jim trampling the Aussies underfoot in an amazing variety of ways. It was the greatest example of media 'hype' since Freddie Trueman had annihilated the Indians four years earlier – and what were the Indians compared with an Australian touring side? And the Old Trafford Test was still to come ...

That game was played on 26, 27, 28, 30 and 31 July, 1956 and it will forever be known as Laker's Match – rightly so, of course. It occupies its own place in Australian folklore, where the emphasis is placed firmly upon the story of an impossible wicket – so let us look at that side of the game first of all. Jim himself often recalled a brief, but significant, conversation with Sir Donald Bradman (back in England as an expert comments man for the *Daily Mail*) on the eve of the Test. As Jim walked

SURREY *v* AUSTRALIA
At The Oval, 16–18 May 1956

AUSTRALIA

J. W. Burke lbw b Laker	28	– c and b Lock	20
C. C. McDonald c Swetman b Laker	89	– c Laker b Lock	45
K. Mackay c Surridge b Laker	4	– lbw b Laker	4
R. N. Harvey c Constable b Laker	13	– c May b Lock	10
K. R. Miller not out	57	– c Swetman b Lock	2
L. Maddocks b Laker	12	– c Laker b Lock	0
R. R. Lindwall b Laker	0	– c Constable b Lock	4
I. W. Johnson c Swetman b Laker	0	– run out	5
A. K. Davidson c May b Laker	21	– c May b Laker	7
P. Crawford b Laker	16	– not out	5
J. Wilson c Swetman b Laker	4	– st Swetman b Lock	1
B 4, l-b 8, n-b 3	15	– L-b 4	4
	259		**107**

1/62 2/93 3/124 4/151 5/173 6/173   1/56 2/73 3/83 4/85 5/85 6/89 7/92
7/175 8/199 9/217   8/101 9/104

Bowling: *First Innings* – Loader 15–4–30–0; Surridge 8–2–8–0; Laker 46–18–88–10; Lock 33–12–100–0; Cox 5–0–18–0. *Second Innings* – Loader 2–2–0–0; Surridge 1–1–0–0; Laker 25–10–42–2; Lock 31.1–9–49–7; Clark 8–4–12–0.

SURREY

D. G. W. Fletcher c Maddocks b Johnson	29	– not out	9
T. H. Clark c Maddocks b Burke	58	– not out	8
B. Constable c and b Johnson	109		
P. B. H. May st Maddocks b Johnson	27		
K. Barrington c Miller b Johnson	4		
R. Swetman st Maddocks b Davidson	0		
D. F. Cox b Davidson	13		
J. C. Laker c McDonald b Johnson	43		
W. S. Surridge c Harvey b Johnson	38		
G. A. R. Lock b Davidson	0		
P. J. Loader not out	12		
B 10, l-b 3, w 1	14	– B 1, l-b 1, n-b 1	3
	347	(No wkt)	**20**

1/53 2/112 3/147 4/192 5/195 6/221
7/278 8/302 9/313

Bowling: *First Innings* – Lindwall 2–1–10–0; Crawford 1–0–4–0; Johnson 60.3–12–168–6; Davidson 44–14–101–3; Wilson 19–9–34–0; Burke 7–2–16–1. *Second Innings* – Lindwall 8–4–8–0; Crawford 7–3–9–0.

Surrey won by 10 wickets

out to look at a pitch which, from the boundary, looked curiously short of grass, he met The Don returning from his own inspection. 'Flat and slow,' was the Bradman verdict, 'with plenty of runs in it.' Within 48 hours of that pronouncement (and there could have been none more authoritative) Australia were considering an official protest about the pitch and Bradman himself led his *Daily Mail* article with this sentence: 'If anyone doubted my forecast that this Test wicket would not last, let him take a look at the scoreboard now.' The *Daily Express*, countering the *Mail*'s enterprise in signing up Bradman by getting comments from Arthur Morris, ran a second-deck headline: 'This wicket is unfit for Test cricket.' Beneath it, Morris's comments ran like this:

I am not going to say the pitch was a nightmare but I have got two main points of criticism. (1) That it should not have shown such advance signs of wear on the first and second days of a five-day match. Surely it is not too much to expect in an international match that the pitch should remain in reasonable condition for the first three days so that both teams can enjoy equable fortune in their first innings? (2) I complain, not on behalf of Australia but on behalf of cricket that the pitch was not properly prepared for a match of this kind. Someone slipped up somewhere and things have not been improved by official statements from the Lancashire club that there was little wrong with the wicket. For a second day there was a great deal wrong with it.

Jack Fingleton, the former Australian opening batsman who afterwards became a brilliant cricket writer and broadcaster, cast the net of responsibility just a little wider. After two days play he offered this view of the situation:

When I saw it for the first time on Thursday I knew it was not a typical Old Trafford pitch. It was brown, and Old Trafford pitches have always had a healthy tinge of green. I wrote about its dry condition, how it would favour spin bowlers. Now I want to qualify some of this in case it is thought that the Australians – as their scores suggest – were confronted with a most difficult pitch. It was nothing of the sort. It was not as good a pitch as one expects on only the second day of a five-day Test but one had only to watch the batting of Sheppard, Evans and even Lock, of England, and then Burke, of Australia, to realise that the Australians put up a most ineffectual display.

Those are contemporary views expressed by experienced and expert observers. In preparing this book I consulted Keith Miller, who in 1956 was the most experienced of the Australian batsmen. This is what he had to say:

Before the game there were smallish cracks in the pitch and the colour was very different – reddish – from anything I had ever seen in the UK.

(This, remember, was Miller's third tour apart from his experience of playing with the Royal Australian Air Force side in 1945, plus a lot of wartime cricket, so he was extremely knowledgeable about English conditions.)

I rubbed my fingers across a portion of the pitch and there was dust on them. I turned to the umpires – Frank Lee and Emrys Davies – and said, 'Well, gentlemen, I reckon this game will end in three days.' And Frank said, 'Keith, I've just said the same thing to Emrys.' England batted first, the pitch played all right, then Laker, as accurate as ever, got big turns. It was years later when I looked at the scores and noted to my great surprise that Colin McDonald made 80-odd in the second dig – quite an innings to have survived.

More from the magnificent Miller in a moment but let us now consider the fact that the burden of most of the Australian criticism we have seen is that the pitch behaved unreasonably on the first two days of the game. In the period up to lunch on the second day, England accumulated 459 with centuries from Peter Richardson and the Rev David Sheppard. The Australian spinners, Johnson and Richie Benaud, returned respective figures of 47–10–151–4 and 47–17–123–2. During the remainder of the second day, Australia were bowled out for 84 and, following on, were 53 for one at the close. Is it possible for the nature of a wicket to change so dramatically in the course of a day? One might almost ask if such a change is possible within the space of a few minutes because it was not until Laker and Lock switched ends – with the off-spinner moving to the Stretford end – that wickets began to fall, and that was just before four o'clock. That there was help for the spinners is undeniable; when a pitch is dry and dusty that is almost invariably the case. But can it possibly be that conditions become *unplayable* at a given moment in late afternoon? Surely not. And can it be coincidence that one fine spin bowler can toil for nearly an hour without success and then find his partner immediately striking oil, so to speak, immediately after changing ends? Again, surely not. The answer has got to lie in an amalgam of factors: (1) That dressing-room ruminations on the state of the pitch – which would certainly *look* strange to Australian eyes – had produced an attitude of suspicion and mistrust, notwithstanding the total of runs the England batsmen had scored on it; (2) the inadequacy of the Australians' batting technique against high-class spin bowling; (3) the arrival of Jim Laker's finest hour in the whole of a distinguished bowling career. Throughout his later life he dwelt lovingly on the memory of the delivery which accounted for Neil Harvey in the first innings, a ball of perfect length which pitched middle-and-leg to the marvellously accomplished left-hander and took the top of the off-stump. So much of spin bowling is about thinking and so much of batting against spin bowling is about counter-thinking that it is surely not over-romanticising the situation to feel that Laker's superb delivery in that first innings played a major psychological part in the second dismissal of Harvey when he came in, late in the day, after McDonald had retired hurt with jarred knee tendons. Jim, having adjusted the field slightly, bowled what he described as his worst ball in the whole match, a slow full toss around the leg stump line – and the best left-handed batsman Laker ever bowled to patted it gently to Colin Cowdrey, at silly mid-on. Harvey had bagged a pair in less than two hours' play.

Richie Benaud, who was to be for so long Jim's television commentary colleague, was very much involved in that Old Trafford Test. He thought it was 'a terrible pitch, but a terrible pitch (I thought so at the time and I still think so) on which England made 459. In view of this, there's not much more one can say except that I did not think it was a good *cricket* pitch'.

Pitches, of course, were left uncovered when it rained in those days and therefore we are talking about conditions largely unfamiliar to modern players and, indeed, the new generation of spectators. A brief, experimental, return to uncovered wickets in 1987 in an attempt to encourage the rebirth of the spinner's art could give little indication of the state of play in the Lock–Laker era because great spin bowlers do not develop in the course of one season and in 1987 the bowlers themselves were operating in unfamiliar conditions. The only real link between the two generations has probably been Derek Underwood, Kent's great left-arm bowler.

Benaud frankly accepts that Australia's batting in the first innings at Old Trafford, 1956, was 'to put the very best light on it, abysmal'. The Aussies simply tried to hit their way out of trouble and it was the wrong method. Laker took nine wickets and Benaud does not begrudge him any one of them while feeling that he and his colleagues did not help their own cause. After the debacle, there were long, grim and earnest discussions in the Australian camp; it was not going to happen again. And now we come to the essential greatness of the Laker achievement as Benaud (who was to become one of the greatest Australian captains and whose brilliance as a commentator makes his the view to be respected, arguably above all others) recaptures the drama of the match for us:

The 10 wickets for Surrey was unbelievable. No one ever thought that would be done against an Australian side. I didn't see it because I had been to a theatre matinée with Neil Harvey and when we came out and bought a paper to see how the match was going we simply couldn't believe it. We went through the Trent Bridge match [drawn] and Lord's, on a green pitch where Miller bowled magnificently [five for 72 and five for 80] and we won. Then it rained at Leeds and we were beaten, having had to follow on. And so we came to Old Trafford. No one had *any* thought of a bowler taking all 10 in a Test despite what had happened at The Oval. Jim's 10 for 53 was incredible, but 19 for 90 in the match was *absolutely* incredible. I can still see Trevor Bailey shaking his head in disbelief as the players came off the field. And I can also see Tony Lock shaking *his* head at the other end!

Jim had bowled very well in the Leeds match [five for 58 and six for 55] and no matter how many times you think about the Old Trafford game it's impossible to come up with many bad balls he bowled. And yet it still seems incredible. In the second innings there were people trying to get down the track to him, people trying to play him off the back foot, people trying to smother the spin ... we had thought long and hard about it and we were trying everything we knew.

Another aspect which might be worth dwelling on is that after 1956 we resolved that when Jim came out to Australia we were going to get after him. He had never played there; the wickets were going to be very different from Old Trafford and we would be waiting for him. We were. And we did get after him. His figures weren't as good as they had been in England but he still topped the tour bowling averages and took most wickets. Now that's the mark of a great bowler. It's not just an ordinary bowler or a very good bowler. It's the mark of a great bowler because the pitches in 1958–59 were good. I bowled on them; I know how good they were. Jim didn't play in one of the Test matches and yet he still topped the figures. 'Great' is a vastly over-used word – but he was a great bowler, in all conditions.

And Trevor Bailey, who left the field shaking his head, looks at it this way: 'I kept repeating to myself that it was all a dream – it could not have happened.'

David Sheppard's favourite after-the-match recollection involves Jim's advertising of Lucozade. As the champagne flowed in the dressing-room and the crowd gathered outside, clamouring for the 19-for-90 man, Jim remembered his contract and, before appearing on the balcony, he remarked, 'I had better advertise the right product.' He poured himself a glass of the energy-inducing drink, walked out and toasted the crowd as they cheered him. A fortnight later when the team gathered at The Oval for the final Test, Jim showed the man who was to become the Bishop of Liverpool a selection from his fan-mail. In terms of deep disgust a whole group of correspondents reminded him how disgraceful it was that a great sportsman should lead young people astray by encouraging them to drink alcohol! And David Sheppard provides us with an example, too, of the dry Laker wit. They stood alongside each other in the gulley at The Oval as Tyson bowled. The fourth ball of the match was whipped off his legs by Colin McDonald and Lock brought off a blinding catch at leg slip. Laker turned to Sheppard with that wry smile and said, 'I haven't really got anything to play for now in this match.'

But back to Old Trafford and a parting shot from Keith Miller:

I saw Bert Flack, the groundsman, as I was leaving the pavilion and asked him if the press had been giving him a hard time about the pitch. He replied, 'Keith, I've been so bloody busy since the game finished that I haven't had time to cut my own bloody throat'.

It has to be recorded, however, that the aggressive little man who prepared that 1956 pitch at Old Trafford steadfastly refused to accept that there was anything wrong with it. If the bloody Australians couldn't play good spin bowling, that was their look-out.

While the first-innings nine-for-37 was being recorded in Manchester, Lilly Laker was busy organising the care of their two young daughters while she enjoyed a week-end with her husband. With no time to switch on the television or radio she had no idea that Jim was a national hero once again so she was startled to find the platform at Warrington (the nearest station to the England team's hotel at Lymm, Cheshire) thronged with photographers. 'Good Lord – what have you been doing?' she asked when she met the new national hero off the train. One of the more pleasant aspects of their extremely public greeting of each other was that the *Daily Mirror* cameraman had a spot of technical trouble as they kissed so it was necessary to go through the clinch all over again.

And then it rained for almost the whole of the Saturday and so Lilly saw only 45 minutes play which, however, took in the wicket of Jim Burke, caught Lock, bowled Laker. It is interesting to reflect, as an aside, how well these two bowlers complemented each other. While Lock, the specialist short-leg (and one of the finest the game has ever known) had a hand in so many of the off-spinner's wickets, Laker, specialising in close-in positions on the off-side held many catches when the slow left-armer was bowling. The Lymm Hotel, under the management of Roger Allen, was one of the England team's favourite watering-holes for many years and while the Lakers spent most of Sunday looking out on lowering, wintery skies they at least were able to enjoy the hospitality of an hotel where the staff looked forward to the five days of the Old Trafford Test as the highlight of their catering year. In the evening, Lilly went back to London — something which both of them always regretted because while Jim was most certainly the toast of English cricket fans at the week-end for his nine-for-37 performance, it was, of course, merely a modest fore-runner of the astonishing display of bowling to come.

The rain had stopped by Monday but with the wicket uncovered over the week-end a dusty pitch had now been succeeded by a wet one. It only needed a burst of sunshine to produce a 'sticky dog', the type of pitch which Australians dreaded. Very occasionally one occurred at The Gabba, in Brisbane, but to most of the tourists a drying pitch was simply a nightmare only experienced during tours of England. For the moment — on Monday, 30 July — they were spared the ultimate horror as rain was succeeded by cold winds and only an hour's play was possible, during which Australia advanced to 84 for two. Tuesday morning was fine and dry but there was still no sun and on a dead pitch the tourists reached 112 for two by lunch. And at that point the sun broke through.

Colin McDonald, Ian Craig and Richie Benaud distinguished themselves in that second innings by resolute batting in difficult conditions, but my personal abiding memory centres on Ken Mackay, the Queensland left-hander. On that 1956 tour he headed the Australian batting averages, scoring 1,103 runs at an average of 52.52, figures which any tourist in any age would normally be delighted to take home. He arrived with the reputation of being obdurate beyond description, a man the Australians themselves regarded as being as difficult to dismiss as Trevor Bailey, and no compliment — or condemnation — could be greater than that. Mackay's reluctance to indulge in any sort of exotic strokemaking had earned him the nickname 'Slasher' and his long periods at the crease were founded firmly on a philosophy of giving the bowler as little chance as possible of getting the ball past the bat. He had made his Test debut at Lord's on 21 June, scoring 38 and 31 but when he went to Headingley he looked rather more uncertain against the turning ball and fell twice to Laker for an aggregate of just four runs. Now, at Old Trafford, suspected fallibility became terrible certainty. As long as I live, I never expect to see a recognised Test batsman look as hopelessly at sea as Slasher Mackay did at Old Trafford. For as long as he batted in each innings he consistently played down the wrong line, unable at first to cope with Laker's subtle variations of length and trajectory and, when the ball pitched, he was in even worse straits at the turn. He groped and flailed, played and missed, in what seemed a horrifyingly naive effort to cope with class spin bowling in helpful conditions. From that whole match − which could scarcely have been more dramatic overall and which produced the most incredible performance by a bowler in the history of Test cricket − whenever the subject is broached, one picture flashes into my mind ... Ken Mackay pursuing those hopelessly unavailing efforts to bat against Jim Laker. Jim himself, years later, wrote:

> I suppose it is not very often that an Englishman holds much sympathy for an Australian, especially in the middle of a tensely fought Test series. But I genuinely felt sorry for Mackay that summer. He was an exceptionally fine player, yet when the ball turned at Leeds and Manchester he looked like a complete novice and made only four runs in four innings. It was hard to believe that this was the same Mackay who had roasted the great Lindwall in his prime and who was still to average 125 in a series in South Africa; the same Mackay who played in more than 100 Sheffield Shield matches and was respected wherever he played.

But it was, it was. And if the determined, phlegmatic Slasher ever suffered from nightmares the most terrifying must have centred on Old Trafford, July, 1956.

Jim's analyses over the two innings read like this: 16.4−4−37−9 and 51.2−23−53−10 − 19 for 90 in the Fourth Test of 1956. It was the first time any bowler had taken all 10 in a Test innings and no one had ever before (or since) taken 19 wickets in a Test Match. English writers, by the end of the match, had run out of superlatives. After Laker's first-innings nine-for-37 performance, there had been an emphasis on the part played by the pitch itself, with the Australian press in the main condemning it as unfit for Test cricket and the English largely refuting such allegations. But at the end of the match that sort of partisanship had to be set aside. The great Australian spin bowler Bill O'Reilly (who had become one of that country's most knowledgeable and outspoken cricket writers) offered this view:

His delicately accurate bowling commended this amazing result on Manchester's friendly pitch. He had the Australians on the run and he went relentlessly on until he had them all back in the pavilion. Spin alone meant little to him. No delivery in this second innings turned far but, allied to direction which had the fall firing away continuously at the stumps, and a control which pitched the ball in the places where it occasionally lifted high, made his spinning irresistible.

Jack Fingleton (after revealing that the entire congregation of the press box broke its most solemn unwritten rule – no partisanship at any time – by rising to clap Laker off the field) wrote as follows:

It must not be thought for an instant that Laker's success was due to this pitch. Have a look at Tony Lock's figures, for instance, and you will see what I mean. Lock did not bowl badly yesterday. He beat the bat a number of times but things just didn't go his way. Once again, it was the Australians who couldn't handle Laker's off-spinners, always on length and always on the stumps, or breaking off the stumps to the leg-trap.

Lindsay Hassett:

He bowled so accurately to his well-placed field that the batsmen almost gave the impression that they were bent on giving practice to the men in the close leg-trap. Ranking high amongst his qualities is a modest, almost self-effacing front he presents on the field in the midst of his triumphs. Many players of lesser ability and performance indulge in showy and temperamental displays but Laker's mind is concentrated on his task. He never wastes a movement.

Neville Cardus:

To the student of the game it was a refreshment to the mind and spirit once again to see classic flight and variation of pace, with spin added – after years of the automatism of seam bowling, in-swinging and all the rest of the contemporary tricks. The Australians, especially, should be grateful to Laker, though overwhelmed by him, for the education he gave to them in a science they have recently neglected.

It is interesting to note here Sir Neville's condemnation of the pre-dominance of seam bowling in the fifties – it is not a purely modern phenomenon.

Sir Donald Bradman:

> I cannot recall any off-spinner who has spun the ball more, at his pace. Flight is not disregarded, though it plays a comparatively unimportant part in his plan of attack. He delivers the ball from about as high a trajectory as one can achieve consistent with maximum spin, using splendid body and shoulder movement. This combination, plus wrist and finger, give him considerable nip. Indispensable to his success is the watertight field to which he bowls. Two leg-slips, another man (very short) about square, mid-on, square-leg on the fence and a deep mid-wicket, sometimes halfway out. The close men take care of pure defence, the outer ring of the swishes, *but the inner circle is the real menace.*

So let us look at Laker's bowling, particularly in the Old Trafford Test, through the eyes of one member of that indispensable inner ring. In the first innings of the game, Alan Oakman caught Miller and Mackay; in the second he disposed of McDonald, Mackay and Ron Archer. The left-hander went to catches at silly-point; the right-handers fell to what is now known as the bat-pad position, but in point of fact Oakman did not start off in that place to the off-spinner. He was a specialist slip who held 594 catches in his first-class career, and the Rev. David Sheppard was originally placed at short square-leg by May, but was quick to point out that as he was returning to the England side in that Test after a long absence his reflexes were not as sharp as he would have liked. May accepted this and asked Oakman, 'Would you mind going in there, Alan?' (My, weren't captains polite in those days? Alan Oakman, however, is clear in his recollection of the request.) There was no objection from the Sussex man: 'I hadn't got any bloody runs so I thought I had better do as I was asked.'

It was Oakman's second Test and it turned out to be his last one – so at least he is able to look back on a memorable little spell at the top. England won both matches in which he took part by an innings and 42 (Headingley) and an innings and 170 (Old Trafford). And he held seven catches in the two matches, all off Laker's bowling. He went on the following winter's tour to South Africa and although he didn't play in a Test he consolidated a firm friendship with Jim. They shared a cabin on the outward voyage which was probably not the best example of billeting ever worked out by a tour management – Laker was well over six foot tall and broad with it; Oakman, while slim, was six foot five. In consequence, they did not spend a great deal of time together in the cabin! Their association, however, went back a long way – to 1947 when they met in a Second XI game between Surrey and Sussex.

Some sort of rapport must have sub-consciously been established between the two of them because in a game at Hove, where Oakman was on a pair when he started his second innings, he recalls that Laker pushed back Bernie Constable at cover and gave him a soft one to get off the mark, a chivalrous gesture which one can't really see being echoed in modern cricket. Oakman responded by smashing Laker over long-on for six in the next over – and JC was not at all amused!

After nearly 500 games for his native Sussex, Oakman joined the Warwickshire coaching staff at Edgbaston and is now assistant secretary (cricket) there. But, going back to Old Trafford, 1956, Oakman's abiding memory is of the Herculean efforts of Tony Lock to get amongst the wickets:

> Don't believe any of those tales about Lockie urging Jim on to all 10. That certainly didn't happen. No one could have tried harder than Tony to get into the frame. He just about worked himself into a frenzy, but the harder he tried, the less likely he seemed to take one. After the game, Jim took his glass of Lucozade out onto the balcony to acknowledge the cheers of the crowd. He was there only a few minutes but by the time he came back, Lockie had changed and left. His natural professionalism told him he ought to have taken wickets on a pitch where his partner had got 19. A great competitor, Tony Lock, in every way.

So what has Lock himself got to say of the occasion?

> None of us expected the wicket to start going as early as the second day. Lindwall and Miller had bowled an over apiece without getting the ball above bail high and Benaud looked up from the outfield at our dressing-room and laughed. It indicated his view that no bowler was going to get much out of this pitch. At that time you could have had any odds you wanted on a drawn game.

(We are certainly getting a number of different views of that Old Trafford pitch.) Back to Lock:

Believe me – conditions in their first innings and ours were not so very different. The fact was that the Australians simply didn't have the spin bowlers to exploit the turf and that Sheppard, Cowdrey and Richardson in particular batted very well. I believe the authorities in both Leeds and Manchester set out to prepare fair wickets which would allow spin bowlers to turn it sooner or later. They just happened to 'go' earlier than expected.

I started at the Stretford end, where Ian Johnson had bowled in the England first innings, but when Jim and I were switched the attack became altogether more effective. Jim had McDonald caught in the leg-trap and then bowled Neil Harvey in the same over. Either that was the key ball in the match or it was the leg-break with which I had Jimmy Burke caught at slip immediately after tea.

(Now we must break off the Lock narrative at this point to take a look at that famous scorecard. With Jim taking 19 wickets in the match and Tony a solitary one, is it not perhaps a manifestation of professional vanity for him to claim that his one wicket might have been a key factor in the game as a whole? Improbable, perhaps, but it is nevertheless possible to make out a case in support of his point. The dismissal of Harvey, following that of McDonald, with that delivery which Laker remembered with such delight for so long after the event, meant that two wickets had fallen at the same total, 48, after the Australian openers had suggested they were going to bat with the same resolution and confidence as England's. Harvey was at the peak of his career and was regarded as probably the most formidable of the Australian batsmen. On the other hand, Burke was a notoriously difficult batsman to dislodge and when Lock had him caught by Cowdrey, three wickets now fell at the same total. It was undoubtedly a significant dismissal and Lock, writing only a year after the actual event, in his book *For Surrey and England*, was almost certainly still smarting at the memory of his one wicket against Jim's 19. It was the only wicket Laker did not take and yet, in the context of the first innings and the Australian expectations of a reasonable reply to England's 459, it was an important one.)

On with the Lock story:

After Burke had gone, Laker then took seven wickets for eight runs in 22 balls. Australia all out 84, after being 48 for one. No one could blame the pitch for Harvey's dismissal in the second innings. He moved out to make an overpitched ball into a full toss and put it straight into Cowdrey's hands at mid-on. There was not another fielder within 20 yards. Harvey uttered a cry of despair and threw his bat high in the air. When Laker had taken six or seven wickets thoughts began to gather in the minds of the players – and the crowd – of his doing the impossible and repeating the all-10 feat he had achieved for Surrey against the Aussies. But I can dismiss any notion that towards the end I eased off to make this possible. There have been occasions when, with only a wicket or two left and the result a foregone conclusion, one bowler has aimed wide so as to allow a colleague to complete an all-10 feat. Peter Loader had done it to help me to all 10 against Kent at Blackheath earlier in 1956. But this was a Test Match against Australia. The Ashes were in the balance and time was pressing. We could not afford to ease up at either end. If I nipped in for a wicket or two it would be bad luck for Jim, but England's interests had to come first. Try as I did, however, the wickets would not fall at my end. I did not strike my best form that day but I bowled as well as I have done on occasions when I have taken six or seven wickets. It so happened on that final day at Manchester that I beat bat and stumps several times but the wickets simply avoided me.

As they walked from the field at the end of it all, the captain had one word of consolation for Lock. Peter May said quietly to him, 'Well bowled, Tony. Forget the scorebook. You played your part, too.' However, from his personal disappointment at not being more prominently involved in a great England bowling occasion, Lock has salvaged one memory with a smile. It is of an attempted piece of gamesmanship by the Australian captain. Seeking to prolong matters by whatever means possible, Johnson (who batted at number 11) complained that sawdust which had been put down to secure the bowlers' footholds was being whipped up by the wind and impairing his vision. He asked that play be halted while the sawdust was swept away. When the appeal was turned down, he prepared to receive the next ball with a philosophical smile: 'Well, at least it's one that Trevor Bailey never thought of.'

On the next page, then, is that historic scorecard in full.

When the tumult and shouting had subsided a little, Jim set out to drive home to Putney. Tomorrow was another day, another game and it was back to duty with Surrey. But in the pre-motorway era it was a long and wearisome drive from Manchester to London and halfway along the trip he decided to stop, shortly before closing-time in the pubs, for a pint and a sandwich. As he stood at the bar enjoying his snack, the television news showed something of the flurry of wickets which had

ENGLAND *v* AUSTRALIA
(Fourth Test)

At Old Trafford, Manchester, 26–31 July 1956

ENGLAND

P. E. Richardson c Maddocks b Benaud	104
M. C. Cowdrey c Maddocks b Lindwall	80
Rev. D. S. Sheppard b Archer	113
P. B. H. May c Archer b Benaud	43
T. E. Bailey b Johnson	20
C. Washbrook lbw b Johnson	6
A. S. M. Oakman c Archer b Johnson	10
T. G. Evans st Maddocks b Johnson	47
J. C. Laker run out	3
G. A. R. Lock not out	25
J. B. Statham c Maddocks b Lindwall	0
B 2, l-b 5, w 1	8
	459

1/174 2/195 3/288 4/321 5/327
6/339 7/401 8/417 9/458 10/459

Bowling: *First Innings* – Lindwall 21.3–6–63–2; Miller 21–6–41–0; Archer 22–6–73–1; Johnson 47–10–151–4; Benaud 47–17–123–2.

AUSTRALIA

C. C. McDonald c Lock b Laker	32	– c Oakman b Laker	89
J. W. Burke c Cowdrey b Lock	22	– c Lock b Laker	33
R. N. Harvey b Laker	0	– c Cowdrey b Laker	0
I. D. Craig lbw b Laker	8	– lbw b Laker	38
K. R. Miller c Oakman b Laker	6	– (6) b Laker	0
K. D. Mackay c Oakman b Laker	0	– (5) c Oakman b Laker	0
R. G. Archer st Evans b Laker	6	– c Oakman b Laker	0
R. Benaud c Statham b Laker	0	– b Laker	18
R. R. Lindwall not out	6	– c Lock b Laker	8
L. V. Maddocks b Laker	4	– (11) lbw b Laker	2
I. W. Johnson b Laker	0	– (10) not out	1
Extras	0	– B 12, l-b 4	16
	84		**205**

1/48 2/48 3/62 4/62 5/62 6/73 7/73
8/78 9/84 10/84

1/28 2/55 3/114 4/124 5/130 6/130
7/181 8/198 9/203 10/205

Bowling: *First Innings* – Statham 6–3–6–0; Bailey 4–3–4–0; Laker 16.4–4–37–9; Lock 14–3–37–1. *Second Innings* – Statham 16–10–15–0; Bailey 20–8–31–0; Laker 51.2–23–53–10; Lock 55–30–69–0; Oakman 8–3–21–0.

England won by an innings and 170 runs.

taken place earlier in the day and he joined the locals in watching with interest England's Test victory. No one recognised him; Laker showed no more or no less fascination than anyone else in the pub and when the news had finished, continued on his way home. Afterwards he laconically remarked that it was rather interesting to have seen himself on television for the first time.

At the house in Portinscale Road the press photographers were waiting for his return, even though it was now well after midnight, and the following morning the telegrams started to arrive, some forwarded from Old Trafford and his county headquarters at The Oval, some direct to the house from friends who knew the home address. They came from tankers, freighters, coasters and Royal Navy ships at sea. One, from H.M.A.S. Albatross where a number of naval petty officers were enjoying an attachment to the Royal Australian Navy, thanked Jim for keeping them in spending money! A few bets with the indigenous complement of the Albatross had obviously paid off well. Cricket clubs from Calcutta to Nyasaland sent their compliments; so did local government officials and dignitaries from Shipley to Surrey County Council. Old boys of his school joined with the Saltaire Cricket Club to express their delight; players like Denis Compton, Alan Wharton, Jackie McGlew (from South Africa) and George Headley and John Goddard (West Indies) cabled their congratulations. One telegram read, 'Gay Nineties Club, 21, Hertford Street, is proud of its record-breaking member,' and in 1989 we had better point out that the adjective has an entirely different connotation from the one it bore in 1956. And, of course, some people are never satisfied: one simply said, 'Congratulations. Why not 20?'

At the end of the year the *Daily Express*'s influential columnist, Desmond Hackett, made Jim his Sportsman of the Year and the (Sunday) *Reynolds News* played a variation on the same theme by nominating Laker its Mr Sport of 1956, pointing out that in a notable year the opposition included Chris Brasher, Terry Spinks, Dick McTaggart, Stanley Matthews, Billy Wright and John Charles.

There remains one other Laker bowling analysis which is very much a part of cricket history — eight wickets for two runs in the Test Trial staged at Park Avenue, Bradford, in 1950. It was indeed a strange choice of venue for such a game because the Bradford wicket, ever a 'sporting' one, could be a death-trap for batsmen if there was rain about, and bearing in mind that the selectors had chosen three of that band of promising youngsters from Cambridge University (Peter May, David Sheppard and Hubert Doggart) and one from Oxford (Donald Carr), it promised to be a severe test of the technical skills of youngsters accustomed to the relative perfection of Fenner's and The Parks. At worst it could kill them off altogether. Jim Swanton remembers asking Brian Sellers if the pitch would be covered before the game and receiving the uncompromising response: 'Covered? They'll play on what they find.' And what they found was a sticky dog which caused J. C. Laker to rub his hands in delighted anticipation as soon as he saw it. He knew the ground well. Park Avenue was the home of the Bradford Cricket Club, at that time a member of the Bradford League, and Laker knew exactly how the pitch would play. Even he, however, must have been mildly surprised by the results he obtained on that first morning.

There was not a full house, by any means, when Norman Yardley, captain of Yorkshire and England, who knew even better than Jim Laker how the wicket would perform, won the toss and put in the relatively inexperienced Rest side. The cricket world, inevitably, is now densely populated with people who insist they were there and saw it all, just as happened after The Oval in 1956 and Old Trafford later that year. But John Arlott, writing at the time, reported a sparse attendance to see Laker quickly take over at the pavilion end after Trevor Bailey had taken the first wicket (David Sheppard, lbw for four). Test trials did not mean very much to Yorkshire folk who didn't mind forking out their hard-earned brass for the real thing at Headingley – but a mere trial at Bradford? Not on your life. The locals knew as well as anyone (and certainly better than the unwary hopefuls of The Rest side) what could happen to the inexperienced batsman on a Park Avenue sticky and I have to confess that while 'up home' from Nottingham where I worked at that time to visit my parents and my in-laws, I didn't bother to go myself. And so I missed a remarkable piece of cricket history. In 14 overs Jim Laker conceded two singles and took eight wickets. One of the singles, moreover, was a 'courtesy', one off the mark in the form of a gentle full toss to his Surrey clubmate, Eric Bedser. The other was scored by the 19-year-old F. S. Trueman and over the years I have been privileged to hear different versions of how this was accomplished. To Jim (if I may paraphrase his actual words) the single was a trifle fortuitous; to Fred, it came as a result of stroke-play of the highest pedigree!

The full scorecard of the match is reproduced on the following page.

With one exception, all the members of that side played for England at some point in their careers and Eric Bedser would certainly have earned a place as an all-rounder in another age. It is worthy of note that Les Jackson, second highest scorer, while being one of the most respected

ENGLAND *v* THE REST

At Bradford, 31 May–1 June, 1950

THE REST

D. J. Kenyon c Evans b Laker	7	– lbw b Hollies	9
D. S. Sheppard lbw b Bailey	4	– b Laker	3
G. H. G Doggart c Bailey b Laker	2	– st Evans b Hollies	2
P. B. H. May c Hutton b Laker	0	– b Laker	2
D. B. Carr c Bailey b Laker	0	– st Evans b Hollies	2
E. A. Bedser lbw b Laker	3	– c Evans b Hollies	30
R. T. Spooner b Laker	0	– c Yardley b Bedser	22
R. O. Jenkins not out	0	– c Bedser b Hollies	3
R. Berry b Laker	0	– c Yardley b Bedser	16
F. S. Trueman st Evans b Bedser	1	– not out	0
L. Jackson c and b Laker	5	– st Evans b Hollies	1
B 3, l-b 1, w 1	5	– B 4, l-b 6, n-b 3	13
	27		**113**

1/7 2/10 3/10 4/10 5/18 6/19 7/20   1/12 2/27 3/32 4/32 5/42 6/84 7/91
8/20 9/21   8/110 9/112

Bowling: *First Innings* – Bailey 6–4–3–1; Bedser 9–3–12–1; Laker 14–12–2–8; Hollies 7–5–5–0. *Second Innings* – Bailey 5–2–6–0; Bedser 9–2–22–2; Laker 18–4–44–2; Hollies 22.4–13–28–6.

ENGLAND

L. Hutton b Trueman	85
R. T. Simpson st Spooner b Berry	26
W. J. Edrich lbw b Jenkins	46
J. D. Robertson c Sheppard b Berry	0
J. G. Dewes c Doggart b Berry	34
N. W. D. Yardley c Trueman b Jenkins	13
T. E. Bailey c Spooner b Berry	7
T. G. Evans run out	1
J. C. Laker not out	6
A. V. Bedser c Jackson b Jenkins	5
W. E. Hollies st Spooner b Berry	4
L-b 1, n-b 1	2
	229

1/59 2/155 3/156 4/162 5/187 6/212
7/214 8/214 9/214

Bowling: *First Innings* – Jackson 12–3–38–0; Bedser 13–0–60–0; Jenkins 10–0–38–3; Berry 32–10–73–5; Trueman 9–3–18–1.

England won by an innings and 89 runs.

bowlers in the game throughout his career, was possessed of batting talents which we might describe as negligible.

When the press gathered for quotes at the end of the day there was a brief but graphic exchange between Laker and Pat Marshall of the *Daily Express* which has been told many times but is worth repeating here as an early indication of Jim's sardonic style of humour:

Marshall: 'Would this be your best performance?'
Laker: 'Well, I haven't done it right often.'

The popular newspapers, with their huge gifts for trivialisation, gave the credit for Laker's performance, almost without exception, to his Aunt Ellen (Mrs Kane) who was reputed to have taken young Jim out to the local playing fields at the age of four and taught him how to bowl! For a more serious assessment we turn, first, to J. M. Kilburn, of the *Yorkshire Post*:

Laker did, of course, bowl his off-spinners beautifully and the pitch was perfectly attuned to him. In his first three overs he took three wickets for no runs, Doggart, May and Carr, all caught in the leg-trap. Thereafter the unlikely turned to the incredible and finally to the fantastic until Laker completed his analysis by a brilliant caught-and-bowled.

And next, John Arlott:

He employed the correct technique, bowling round the wicket and never indulging in the higher curves of flight which might allow a batsman to move down the pitch to him. But, bowling through a tight arc, he varied his spin, creating doubt in the mind not only of the batsman facing him but also the man at the other end – and those watching from the pavilion – by making the occasional ball, though apparently spun as sharply as its predecessor, flick away outside the off-stump. From behind the arm it was apparent that he never bowled a loose ball: his line was meticulously precise and his combination of length and turn was such that he often compelled and defeated a full-stretch forward defensive stroke. It made a farce of the game as a Test Trial but it showed Laker in the ruthless destroying vein that was to distinguish many of his subsequent performances.

It was a serious blow for the selectors who had realised after 1948 that the West Indies were no longer a second-rate power in international cricket with Stollmeyer followed in the batting order by Worrell, Weekes

and Walcott. The bowling might not, as yet, be comparable in strength —
no one was prepared for the shock of Ramadhin and Valentine that
summer — but it was already clear that a side of full strength had to be
assembled to receive the tourists. Looking for new middle order batsmen,
the selectors' plans were in total disarray after the Bradford trial. Laker
played in the First Test which was won by England at Old Trafford; he
did not play in the remaining three — which were all won by the West
Indies — at Lord's, Trent Bridge and The Oval, and by massive margins,
too. It is true that Laker took only one wicket in the two West Indian
innings at Old Trafford, but with no off-spinner in the side in the
remaining three Tests it is worth noting that Allan Rae, the left-handed
batsman, scored 106, 24, 68, 46 not out and 109.

THE
BRADFORD
LAD

James Charles Laker was born on 9 February, 1922 in a terraced house in Frizinghall – a place-name which fascinated me as a child, when I saw it proclaiming the last station of the six on the nine-mile railway line from Keighley. For years I assumed it indicated some obscure branch of the wool textile trade which provided so many of the words in my boyhood vocabulary. It was only after consulting the reference library in Bradford that a very ancient origin indeed was revealed – pre-Conquest, pre-Danelaw: Frizinghall was, in fact, the Frisian's nook of land.

But, born there in 1922, young Laker would have been very much more conscious of textiles than concerned with Old English. His skyline bristled with woollen mill chimneys in every direction as far as the eye could see, though not all of them would have belched out smoke consistently, six days a week, as the industry struggled to re-establish itself less than four years after the end of the Great War. This was the Bradford of J. B. Priestley, the centre of the wool trade world-wide, a town of great markets with stalls selling twopenny helpings of meat-and-potato pie from huge dishes of the stuff; a town producing the best fish-and-chips the world has ever seen; a town of wonderful, warm, friendly and hospitable people. And Bradford gave its name to a cricket league which has consistently produced more players for county and Test sides than any other comparable unit anywhere in the world.

Jim was born into a family without a trace of sporting history, but in the 19 years until he joined the Army he grew up in an area where sport was a way of life. Every youngster played cricket – boys and girls alike – on any piece of open ground which could be found and with whatever equipment could be improvised. In winter, boys played either football or one of the codes of rugby (union or league) with Bradford City as their soccer idols. The Valley Parade ground was a gentle walk from the first home Jim knew and a modestly priced tram ride from the next family establishment in Baildon, four miles away. Up to the age of five he was taken by his mother to the school where she taught, placed as unostentatiously as possible in one corner and urged to keep quiet while Mum got on with her job. One way and another, Jim must have spent more time in school than almost any contemporary; it is reasonable to speculate that the length of time per day that he spent 'keeping quiet' between the ages of two and five played some part in shaping the essentially reserved nature of the man in his adult life.

Although he was 'sporting mad' as a boy, it is possible that Jim's first hero was not a sportsman at all, but a member of the choir at St Barnabas'

Church, Heaton – a neighbouring suburb of Bradford – where the young Laker made something of a name for himself as a boy soprano. The leading tenor in the church choir was one Arthur Servent who graduated from local oratorio to grand opera and it is a name I remember well from my own boyhood when the choir weekend was a major event in the calendar of most West Riding churches and chapels – a 'secular' concert on Saturday night, followed by 'The Messiah' on Sunday and it brought to our corner of Yorkshire at one time or another some of the top names in British music – Isobel Baillie, Stiles Allen, Frank Titterton, Frank Mullings, Norman Lumsden and Norman Allin. Servent became one of the country's leading singers and who is to say how the young Laker might have developed if he had followed the lead of that first hero. Jim was a soloist not only at St Barnabas but in the school choir at Salts Boys' High School where, his lifelong friend Fred Robinson remembers, his party-piece was Schubert's 'Die Forelle'.

Jim was the fifth child of a formidable lady who spent 50 years as an uncertificated schoolteacher and who emerges from the young Laker's recollections and those of his childhood friends as a person of strong character. Unqualified teachers were not unusual in the 1920s and lack of paper qualification by no means indicated lack of knowledge or the ability to impart it. Indeed, my own first five or six years of education were carried out by a lady of uncertain age whose qualities I would place far above those of many teachers I know personally today, so it is not difficult to visualise the personality of the lady who became Mrs Laker when she married her second husband. He was a stonemason who had come north from his native Sussex to follow his trade, a reversal of the path to be taken later by his son – who never knew him. Jim was always told by his mother and sisters that Charles Laker had died when Jim was two or three years old. Otherwise he was never spoken of and no photograph existed of him. Mr Laker had, apparently, a roving eye or, perhaps, little taste for life in a house with as many as five women. Perhaps it may have been a combination of both which drove him away. As far as his family in the Bradford area were concerned, he was dead. It was, therefore, something of a shock for Jim to learn – only in 1983 – that his father lived on after his departure from the matrimonial home and developed a completely new life. His discovery came as a result of one of those strange turns that Life, with a capital L, occasionally takes.

After retiring from first-class cricket in 1972, Peter Parfitt (the Middlesex and England left-hand batsman) went into business in the north of England by buying a pub in a tiny hamlet midway between

Skipton, gateway to the Yorkshire Dales, and Colne, just over the border in Lancashire. The pub had a semi-derelict barn and other outbuildings which Parfitt converted and rebuilt until he had the most magnificent establishment in the area – a country pub in a delightfully rural setting with not only a dining-room but a ballroom and banqueting suite. When not in use for annual or other dinners, the suite was put to use by Parfitt staging sportsmen's evenings for various charities – he is a dedicated worker for SPARKS, for instance – and at one of these the speaker was to be J. C. Laker, a founder-member and first chairman of SPARKS. When this was announced, Parfitt received a phone call from a man called Norman Petty, a noted spin bowler in local (Ribblesdale League) cricket and an accountant in the neighbouring town of Barnoldswick. He wanted a ticket for the evening but casually inquired, in passing, if Parfitt knew that Laker *père* was buried in a local churchyard. 'Are you sure?' asked Peter, who had never heard Jim refer to his father. 'Certainly,' replied Mr Petty. 'I'll show you the grave if you like. It's in Gill Churchyard.' Twenty minutes later, Detective Parfitt was looking at the last resting place of Charles Laker, stonemason, plus two ladies of another name, one of whom was presumably the lady with whom he had lived 'over the brush' in local parlance and the other, their daughter – a half-sister Jim had never known existed. Not knowing any of this family history in detail, Parfitt (in telephoning Jim Laker to confirm arrangements for the sportsmen's evening and giving detailed advice on how to get to the Tempest Arms, Elslack) idly mentioned: 'Your father is buried only about 10 or 15 minutes drive from my place.' There was silence at the other end of the phone until Jim said, 'I never knew my father' and the call ended with Parfitt feeling a trifle embarrassed.

When the day arrived for the sportsmen's evening, he greeted his guest with an apology which Jim interrupted with a counter-apology, explaining that he had been told since early childhood that his father had died when Jim was three years old so he had been rather taken by surprise. Then he asked, 'Can you take me to see the grave?' And so, as he stood in a churchyard in a tiny corner of Yorkshire he had never previously visited, Jim (then past his 60th birthday) learned just a little about the father he had never known.

There seems no doubt that the Charles Laker buried at Barnoldswick was indeed Jim's father who had died in 1932. As Norman Petty died in 1986 it has not been possible to research the matter beyond the point to which Peter Parfitt has taken us. I would very much have liked to ask Mr Petty how he knew that Charles Laker was the father of the Jim

Laker. It cannot have been parental pride asserting itself when Jim moved into cricketing legend because he was, in fact, only 10 when his father died. Detective Parfitt, however, took his investigation a stage further by tracing the death certificate which revealed that Charles Laker's early death was accelerated by the inhalation of stone-dust and chippings. He had worked for Sir Amos Nelson, a cotton magnate, whose stately home, Gledstone Hall, was close to Barnoldswick – as a stonemason. So the clues certainly seem to point in the right direction and indeed Jim himself was satisfied that he had found his father's grave.

If he missed the guiding hand of a father it was never evident in the adult personality of Jim Laker. Indeed, he was always so much a man's man that it is difficult to think of him as being brought up in a house with five women! But how did that discovery, late in life, that during the first 10 years of his life he had a father living just 25 miles away, affect him? Did he brood on the father-and-son relationship he might have enjoyed and never did? Did he think wistfully of the way his schoolfriends were able to watch football and cricket in parental company when he could not? Did he perhaps resent the fact that knowledge of a living father had been kept from him? It seems probable that the answer to all these questions is 'no'. Jim was never an overtly sentimental or demonstrative man; his memories of his mother held the same gentle affection and respect he had shown as a boy; and his relationships with his sisters remained warm and friendly. A secure and loving family circle gave Jim a confidence which later was to be a great asset – and, just occasionally, something of a disadvantage. He anticipated, for instance, an egalitarianism in cricket for which the game, at that time, was not quite ready. Jim Laker played in the days of amateurs and professionals, gentlemen and players, when neither side was in any doubt about its status and quite fundamentally he resented the fact that there was a difference between the two. If, in the Army, he had joined an infantry regiment (or any unit where a measure of 'bull' was accepted as routine and where officer-other ranks relationships were sharply defined) he might have been able to accept amateur captains in cricket more easily than he did. But the Royal Army Ordnance Corps, and within it Jim's clerkly duties, didn't help him towards that sort of attitude. As a cricketing other rank he was, no doubt, a bit bolshy.

No hint of this comes down to us from his childhood (other than the fact that he grew up without a father's fond discipline) and the first manifestation appears in his career with Surrey. One point the two of us sometimes discussed in detail was that children brought up in our day and our environment learned quite naturally to respect authority, whether it was vested by virtue of position or simply because those older than us were automatically deemed to be wiser. We reached emphatic agreement that any betrayal of our juvenile respect, any indication that faith had been misplaced, was likely to lead to a dramatic change of attitude from one extreme to the other. Respect was quickly replaced by contempt and that could be a rather dangerous transformation. It might explain some of Jim's brushes with authority in the 1950s.

But the principal characteristic which emerges from Jim Laker's youth is very much one of loyalty – to his friends, his cricket mates, his colleagues and, in due course, his family. He first met Fred Robinson, for instance, when they started their first term at Salts Boys' High School. Saltaire was a model village built five miles from Bradford by Sir Titus Salt, the mill-owner whose Victorian paternalism was copied in Cheshire by the first Lord Leverhulme. Port Sunlight was built on soap; Saltaire was built on wool, its streets of identical architecture, providing homes for mill-hands which were ahead of their time by comparison with the average working-class housing in the late 19th century. Saltaire had its own hospital, shops and school as well as the great factory beside the River Aire in the valley bottom.

The first step on the way ahead for a boy of the next century who hoped to progress beyond his own environment was to get a place in a grammar school and the way to do this was to win a county minor scholarship awarded by the West Riding Education Committee (in due course a county major scholarship could take him to university). Jim did this in 1932 to the immense delight of his mother and so began what he often described as seven of the happiest years of his life. The friendship he formed with Fred Robinson was still flourishing when Jim died in 1986. Together they played in the school football team (Laker inside left, Robinson centre or wing-half) and the cricket eleven, occasionally clashing in house-matches like the one ruefully recalled by Fred in which his team were bowled out for one run – Laker six for none, bowling fast, Richard Sutton four for one. Together they progressed to play for Calverley in the Bradford Amateur Football League and for Saltaire in the Bradford League. Fred remembers the schoolboy Laker in a series of staccato sentences of which Jim himself in his later commentary days would probably have approved: 'Very positive. Colourful vocabulary. Very supportive.'

Together they went to the recruiting office in Lady Lane, Leeds, in 1941 to volunteer for war service. Fred was determined on the Royal

Navy and wanted Jim to enlist in the senior service, too, but the young Laker was adamant that it had to be the R.A.O.C. It seems (to someone who a year later was thinking on similar lines about volunteering for the RAF) a very strange choice. Men joined the Royal Navy because of a love of the sea or a definite commitment to that branch of the services. Before, during and since the war I have always regarded naval types as rather special people. Many youngsters of that time found the glamour of the RAF appealing – the Battle of Britain, the bombing of Germany which, in 1941, was just beginning to build up, the uniform which alone in the three services allowed the wearing of a collar and tie! If one felt a strange but compelling urge to go for the Army at all, then what about the 'local' regiment, the Duke of Wellington's or one of the other Yorkshire infantry units? But the Royal Army Ordnance Corps? It seems the most baffling choice for a volunteer. Are we, then, seeing the first glimpse of Laker's desire to be a professional sportsman? One of the major R.A.O.C. depots was at Chilwell, near Nottingham, and on the military grapevine it was strongly rumoured that if you played a game, or a musical instrument, you could find a job for life there. Well, it didn't quite work out as smoothly as that ...

Fred was accepted by the Royal Navy and told to go home and await his call-up in about six months time. Jim returned from the Army end of the recruiting office, visibly shaken, to tell his friend that his instructions were to 'report back next Monday'! After six weeks' basic training he was duly posted to Chilwell right enough, but within a few more weeks he had been issued with tropical kit and after seven days embarkation leave he was on his way to the Middle East. It was here that he learned the skills which were to make him into England's greatest off-spinner. It was here that he met the girl who would become his wife. It was here that he met (and played alongside or against) first-class cricketers who had previously been just names in newspapers and record books to young Laker. Service in the R.A.O.C. reshaped his destiny.

But let us return for a moment to the boyhood days, because this is where Jim and I found much common ground. Mercifully, we were both the children of parents who made sure that the 'hungry thirties' were not hungry for us, but with limited opportunities offering themselves for us to progress outside our own environment, a grammar school education opened up a future which at least held out the prospect of avoiding going directly from school into t'mill. The curriculum, the teaching, the reading in a grammar school not only dangled more inviting prospects before one; they positively kindled the flame of ambition.

Growing up and going to school just five miles apart at roughly the same time, the Laker experience was my experience, and the only major difference in our teenage lives lay in our winter games – association football for Jim, rugby football for me. In the 1980s he could reel off the names of the Bradford City team of the mid-thirties and soccer, in fact, was his first love in those early years.

But cricket was by far the most pleasant way of passing the time between football seasons and his development was quietly noted by the local Bradford League club, Saltaire. He joined them at 15, was in the first team by the time he was 16 and was taken under the wing of a man who was to be a life-long friend. Alf Burgoyne, now aged 87, was secretary of Saltaire CC for 50 years, captain of the second team for 14 years, and still can't let go: he was Saltaire's president in 1988. When I wrote to David Warner, cricket correspondent of the *Bradford Telegraph and Argus,* for help in this area of research he replied, quite simply, 'Alf Burgoyne *is* Saltaire Cricket Club.' And while many others have obviously played their part, it is a fairly safe bet that none of them would argue with that description.

Mr Burgoyne was, in fact, born at Pleasley, in Nottinghamshire, and his earliest introduction to first-class cricket was at Trent Bridge. He is the sort of cricket *aficionado* whose eyes sparkle at the ever-fresh memory of arriving at the ground to see England beaten in two days by Warwick Armstrong's touring Australians in 1921 and finding an empty ground for the last rites. 'Because there was nobody there,' he chortles, '*I* was able to field a ball on the boundary and chuck it back to Jack Gregory.'

Once he had moved to Saltaire, it did not take Alf Burgoyne long to become as dyed-in-the-wool, cantankerous, opinionated a Yorkie as it is possible for anyone to be who was born outside the broad acres. 'In 1945,' he recalls in a moment of wondrous heresy, 'I saw Jim score 57 in a match against Pudsey St Lawrence when Len Hutton got 52, and I know which of 'em I would have picked.' This was seven years after Hutton had scored 364 against the Australians at The Oval and the match he was talking about was one in which Leonard in fact carried his bat through the innings for 52 not out! But that is part of the Bradford League cricket philosophy – my club, right or wrong. Jim had got his half-century for Saltaire and it didn't much matter what anyone had done for Pudsey.

To put this sort of attitude in context it is necessary to look in some depth at the Bradford League which – there can be no argument about it – has for nearly a century been a most prolific production line for first-class players. The West Indian island of Barbados might put up some sort of argument in terms of a number of Test players of outstanding quality but it simply cannot match the sheer volume of products who have gone out into the world of county and international cricket from an area considerably smaller. If one starts with Sutcliffe, Hutton, Close, Illingworth, there are three England captains and one who might have been if the game had been ready for professional leaders before the Second World War. While the League was channelling a continuous supply of players to the county side in the post-war years, the overflow was spilling out to Derbyshire, Warwickshire, Northamptonshire, Somerset – even to Lancashire!

The Bradford League's record as a nursery for county cricketers is quite unique and the very nature of its fiercely competitive cricket leaves its mark on the character and personalities of its products. Verily, they don't 'laik it for fun' in those parts. Jim Laker was a product of that cricket and it showed in every facet of his character throughout his career. He was a malleable teenager and was moulded accordingly. 'He was a very willing sort of lad at 16,' according to Alf Burgoyne. 'Even when he was established in the first team, if I asked him to turn out in a game for t'seconds when t'firsts weren't playing, he'd do it. Anything you asked him to do, he'd do willingly.' As the club secretary, Alf quickly found that the youngster was not short of family backing. Jim's mother wanted him to play for Baildon Green, a rival club, but because he was friendly with a man called George Hayley, who was a Saltaire player, Laker opted for the club on the other side of the River Aire – and Alf received an immediate and peremptory phone call from Mrs Laker: 'He's a good cricketer and he wants putting in t'first team.' For those unfamiliar with idiomatic West Riding speech, 'wants' means quite simply and unequivocally, 'should be'.

It was as a batsman that Jim developed at Saltaire. He bowled a partly optimistic medium-pace and his height enabled him to get a bit of bounce, but if spin bowling had entered his thoughts at the age of 16, 17 or 18 he lacked the physical ability to turn the ball prolifically. Nevertheless, he had his moments, notably one in 1941 when he had not yet joined the Army but the war had enabled several Bradford League clubs to enlist the services of county players while the county championship was suspended 'for the duration'. Saltaire had the two Derbyshire pace bowlers, Bill Copson and Alf Pope, as well as that accomplished all-rounder, Leslie Townsend, from the same county, who bowled off-breaks at around medium-pace. Copson and Pope were averaging around 80 wickets apiece in a season when Saltaire went right through without losing a single match and after a summary dismissal at Roberts Park, the Great Horton captain Edgar Robinson, grimly promised the opposition, 'Just wait till we get you to Great Horton. We'll show you how to play fast bowling.' And for three days before the return match skipper Robinson and his allies watered their pitch assiduously to take every last trace of pace out of it.

Came the day – 12 July, remembered with glee by Alf Burgoyne – and the Derbyshire trio had not arrived at the ground when the clock showed 2.30. Instead, a policeman brought the news that Copson, Pope and Townsend were stranded in Chesterfield where their car had broken down. They were trying to get it repaired but Saturday afternoon in wartime Britain did not offer much hope of that being done. 'What do you want to do?' asked the Great Horton captain. 'D'you want to borrow some substitute fielders?'

'No,' was the Saltaire reply. 'If we need subs we'll get them from our own supporters but the team as selected stands and we'll hope the other three can get here.' Now if this exchange sounds unnecessarily terse to those more gently nurtured in their cricketing youth, let it be said at once that it was a perfectly normal Bradford League exchange – no quarter asked or given. The Derbyshire men did not, in fact, arrive. The sun came out, started to dry the saturated pitch, and J. C. Laker and G. A. Wilson bowled out Great Horton for 103 in reply to Saltaire's 209 for seven to win the match and complete the double. Jim was hardly beyond the experimental stage as a slow bowler; George A. Wilson, who had 15 games for Yorkshire between 1936 and the outbreak of war as a slow left-armer, had a first-class record of one wicket for 138 runs in that time. The pitch-waterers, and the sun which dried it out, had done their work well. It probably provided the first example of Jim Laker combining with a left-arm spinner to roll a side over.

Alf Burgoyne, in the meantime, had picked up one or two good Yorkshire characteristics. While Jim was taking 19 Australian wickets for 90 at Old Trafford in 1956, Alf – then a knitwear and hosiery salesman – watched most of the performance free of charge, on a television set in the window of a shop in West Hartlepool! His close involvement with the Laker career is perhaps best shown by a set of Jim's figures for Saltaire he unearthed at the drop of a hat:

Age	Season	Runs	Avge	Wkts	Avge
16	1938	38	2.8	21	28.2

17	1939	76	8.5	32	23.2
18	1940	257	29.7	7	33.8
19	1941	90	18.0	10	10.4

The 1940 season included a highest score of 101 not out.

From that point, the Laker story belongs, first, to the Army, and then to first-class cricket, but let us look for a moment at Jim's brief return to the north in 1945 which occurred, sadly, through the death of his mother. On Bank Holiday Saturday he declined to play for Saltaire but was persuaded to turn out the following Monday in the match against Pudsey St Lawrence, one of the most consistent of powers in the league's existence. It resulted in a four-wicket defeat for Saltaire but not before young Laker had impressed with that innings of 57, referred to by Alf Burgoyne as 'better than Hutton's'! Do we still have loyalty and partisanship to match that? Of course we do – at least in the Bradford League.

THE ARMY AND AFTER

Jim's wartime voyage to Egypt seemed, 30 or 40 years later, like a great adventure – but at the time it was nothing of the sort. With Hitler's U-boats prowling the oceans, eight weeks at sea was a terrifying experience, even with a convoy escort of an aircraft carrier, a battleship and a flotilla of destroyers. In the other-ranks section, everyone had to be below decks from 5 p.m. until the following morning, and with 300 men sharing 20 wash-basins and toilet facilities it would not have been the most pleasant way to travel even in conditions of calm, which was by no means the case as they zig-zagged their way southwards to Durban via Freetown (Sierra Leone). The four days in South Africa produced what Jim described as 'conditions of unadulterated luxury' and whetted his appetite (as they did for so many other wartime servicemen) to visit that country again in happier circumstances.

But at least, once in Egypt, he knew that he was going to be quartered with a non-combatant unit while more violent and momentous events took place in the western desert, not too far away 'up the line'. He had landed, in his own words, 'a cushy number' and his commonsense told him to make the most of it by plunging into the offduty sporting activities which were available. Having spent some time in the area myself, I can readily vouch for the fact that to be able to enjoy organised games – either as practitioner or spectator – was a godsend and it was as a footballer that Jim first made his mark, rising to the ranks of the British Army XI where he played alongside men like Tom Finney, one of Preston North End and England's all-time greats, and other stars of the English (and Scottish) first divisions. Notwithstanding the fact that it is pretty warm in Egypt most of the year round, the seasons were clearly divided (good, orderly, British colonialism) and it was not until 1942 that he had his first game of cricket abroad.

For a moment we must now backtrack to Jim's teenage years when his close friendship with Fred Robinson was also shared by a man called Harry Dolphin, who was nearly twice the age of the other two but was mad-keen on cricket – a not-unexpected characteristic since he was the nephew of Arthur Dolphin, a major figure in Yorkshire's dynasty of wicketkeepers, who reigned from 1905 to 1927. Harry had spent hours talking cricket to Jim and Fred, passing on the folklore of Yorkshire cricket and becoming something like an elder brother to the two younger men. In fact he was so upset when Jim was posted overseas that he volunteered for duty abroad himself, hoping somehow to catch up with his young friend in the vast military complex of the Middle East! Sadly, his troopship was torpedoed and along with hundreds of others, Harry was listed as 'missing, presumed drowned'.

In those four years of close companionship, Harry Dolphin had not only regaled his two young friends with tales of George Herbert Hirst, Herbert Sutcliffe and Emmott Robinson; he had bowled with them, batted with them and discussed detailed theories of the game, putting forward at one stage the idea that Jim might try bowling off-spin. It was, as Jim himself reflected at times, a strange three-cornered friendship, for men in their thirties do not often opt to spend much of their leisure time with teenagers; moreover young men still at, or just out of, school rarely show a willingness to spend long hours listening to their elders. Strange or not, it was a relationship which gave England its greatest off-spin bowler because, with cricket now beginning in Egypt, the 20-year-old Laker remembered his friend's suggestion. Cricket in his new surroundings was played on matting and that could be death to the medium-pace bowler. It could, on occasions, be exploited by bowlers of genuine pace and, especially if the coir matting was not drawn completely taut, give startling assistance to spinners. It was something I learned to my personal cost during service in India and one touring side in Hong Kong collectively bit the dust when faced by a Chinese leg-spinner who turned out to be the son of the groundsman – the man who pegged down the matting! But in typical methodical Laker fashion, Jim spotted this at once and after briefly enjoying the luxury of turning the ball prodigious distances with a slack matting, he set out to learn his new trade thoroughly in the most disadvantageous conditions possible. Remember, if you will, that there was no coach around to help; there was no good-class off-spinner at hand to advise; there were no coaching manuals or spin-bowling text books to consult. J. C. Laker, off-spinner extraordinary, was completely self-taught.

In no time at all he was taking wickets in inter-unit matches and a haul of eight for 30 in a match at the Gezira Sporting Club (known to thousands of servicemen) got him into a higher sphere of cricket. Suddenly this young man who had had a brief apprenticeship in Bradford League cricket was playing alongside Dudley Nourse from South Africa, Bert Sutcliffe, Don Taylor and Tom Pritchard from New Zealand, and Peter Smith (Essex), Norman Yardley (Yorkshire), Tom Dollery (Warwickshire) and George Emmett (Gloucestershire). While Don Taylor's best years were still ahead of him, Bert Sutcliffe and Tom Pritchard had already played first-class cricket in their own country and the four Englishmen were established county players at home, while Dudley Nourse had made a tour to England with the 1935 South African side. Young Laker was already in distinguished company and he at last permitted himself the wild hope that once back home he might 'just have an outside chance' of playing county cricket.

Fortunately for posterity, the Laker family were avid collectors of newspaper cuttings and other memorabilia which were carefully stored away in scrapbooks. Successes with this new style of bowling fill a complete exercise book – as recorded in 1944 – of snippets from newspapers like the *Egyptian Gazette* (well known to a generation of ex-servicemen) and in publications at home. Mother and sisters were as conscientious in snipping pieces out of their newspapers as Jim was himself in the Middle East. Jim is referred to in many of them as 'Jimmy', a diminutive which none of his later colleagues and friends can ever recall using, and, in a couple of instances, as 'Jack'. But nothing, it seems, escaped the cutting-collecting net; some are merely line-scores of innings or bowling performances but in many of the others, young Laker was already making headlines: 'Laker's Seven Wickets for 9', 'Saltaire cricketer Makes Name for Himself', 'Jack Laker's Big Share in Cairo Win', 'Laker's Six Wickets and Quick 48', and most frequent of all, 'Another Win for C.O.P.O.', Jim's unit side.

From this era comes one of Jim's favourite stories and it is one which in so many ways is typical of the man. His first taste of 'international' cricket was a two-day match in 1944, when Rommel had been safely rolled back across North Africa into Italy, between sides representing England and Australia. It was played at the newly opened Alamein Stadium, commemorating the great desert victory of October 1942, in front of a khaki-clad crowd of 10,000. After a day in the field, Corporal Laker was making his weary way back to his billet across the Kasr-el-Nil Bridge, humping his kit on his back, when a staff car pulled up and a brigadier offered the startled and astonished NCO a lift. As they drove into Cairo the brigadier asked where Jim had come from and was told 'Alamein'.

'Tell me,' was the next question, 'what's the position there now?'

'Well, sir,' replied Jim, 'Australia were 320 for eight at close of play but we missed a few chances.'

At that point, the story goes, the officer turned a nasty purple, ordered the driver to stop and turfed out the passenger on, presumably, the grounds of not-so-dumb insolence. Now it's a nice story and one hesitates to knock it down, but the implication that a senior officer thought that hostilities might still be going on nearly two years after they had been successfully concluded is just a little too much to stomach. What is significant in the tale as Jim used to tell it is that it gives us the clearest possible indication of a deep-seated dislike (perhaps contempt is not too strong a word) of authority. It is an attitude we shall see again in this story. One does not presume to make a judgement on the rights or wrongs of the attitude; it is, however, necessary to draw attention to it because it undoubtedly played a significant part in the life of Jim Laker.

In April, 1945, with the war in Europe nearing its end and Jim now a 23-year-old bachelor, unlikely to be demobilised for some time even when the finish did actually come, he was granted a month's leave in England and returned to a small, terraced house near the Valley Parade football ground of Bradford City. The comfortable home he had left in Baildon had gone with the death of his stepfather (his mother's third husband) but Mum, now 67, was still teaching and had actually refereed a football match at school on the day before Jim arrived. Not surprisingly he found her tired and frail and he rarely left her side as the month at home flew by. With just a few days left, his mother suggested he go to Eastbourne to visit one of his sisters, and she went with him to the station. By the time Jim reached Eastbourne his mother had collapsed and died.

Jim's sense of loss was tremendous, the more so since he had never known his father. He remembered the way his mother had encouraged him in his sporting schooldays in the way a father would have done and knew her for a sound psychologist as well as a kind and generous parent. He recalled the visit to Herbert Sutcliffe's sports outfitter's shop in Leeds, once he had made the first team at Saltaire, and the purchase of a Stuart Surridge bat (£2 five shillings) and a complete outfit of boots, socks, shirt, batting gloves and even a box! But the most staggering item of all was a pair of real buckskin pads. It is extremely unlikely that any other 16-year-old in the Bradford League in 1938 would have had his own pads, let alone a pair made from the finest material available. Jim treasured them and used them throughout his entire first-class career with Surrey and England.

It was Mum who paid for his coaching in Herbert Sutcliffe's winter school at Headingley – which must have meant sacrificing something important in the family budget. He thought of all this now and his memory went right back to the earliest days when she had carried him to her own school and parked him in a corner of the classroom. It was a profoundly sad moment in Jim Laker's life and so he doubly resented the battle he now faced with the army to get his leave extended by two weeks to attend his mother's funeral. To return after that to his unit in Egypt for a matter of months before final repatriation seemed a matter of supreme folly. (A few of us at that time shared similar sentiments about similar experiences.) But there was at least one great compensation for Jim in the news that he had been selected to play in a cricket team representing Middle East Forces against one from Central Mediterranean Forces in Rome. Before returning to his unit, Jim heard Gigli sing 'Cavalleria Rusticana' at the Rome Opera House and paid a highly informal and entirely unauthorised visit to Naples with Bert Sutcliffe and Don Taylor. Finally, the three of them hitched a lift on an RAF Transport Command Dakota to Malta, Tobruk and ultimately Cairo amidst a cargo of fresh fruit – such was the unreal atmosphere of those post-war months with everyone waiting with undisguised impatience for his 'number to come up'.

This was probably the most frustrating time of our lives for all of us in a similar position but, of course, our return to civilian life in a Britain rigged for the strictest austerity had to be accomplished in an orderly and graduated fashion. The waiting period took Jim to Leeds, then Folkestone until he was able to wangle a War Office posting in London in what was to be one of the most significant moves of his life.

Permitted to arrange his own billet, he found digs in the home of an army pal of long standing, Colin Harris, and stayed for five years – long after his demobilisation – in what he once described as 'the closest-knit and happiest family I have ever known'. Even more important for his long-term future, he joined Catford Cricket Club and it was here that his ability was noted by Surrey. They invited him to play in a trial match.

Now it is worth noting that at this stage of his life, notwithstanding his success in Army cricket, Jim was far from sure that he was good enough to make the game a full-time occupation. His upbringing in the hard times of Yorkshire in the thirties, his whole outlook on life as a result of those earlier years, screamed out warnings that 'a steady job with a regular wage' was infinitely more desirable than the rather risky occupation of a professional cricketer. Was he good enough? he asked himself. His doubts in this respect were almost certainly founded on his experience when called to the Yorkshire nets as a promising 16-year-old player with Saltaire. With an offer of 10 shillings a day, plus travelling expenses, he joined about 70 youngsters in the nets at Headingley to be checked for signs of potential greatness by the county coaches and quickly came to the conclusion that about 30 or 40 of them were better players than he was. Now this is a self-assessment of rare honesty. I know literally scores of men who, as boys, were called to the Yorkshire nets but only the merest handful have ever agreed that they were not quite up to the mark. I have, however, heard every hard-luck story in the book: 'Never got a real chance to show what I could do' ... 'had the wrong bloke watching me' ... 'put me to bowl against the three best batsmen in the place' ... 'put me to bat against the three best bowlers' ... 'didn't like my action' ... 'didn't like my take-away with the bat' ... 'said I was no good if I didn't move the ball away from the bat' ... 'said I was no good if I couldn't play the cover-drive like Hutton'. The list is endless. But very, very few have ever said, 'I realised that 30 or 40 were far better players than I was.'

Now what has to be remembered when considering Laker's modest view of his ability at that time – just as it most certainly has to be remembered when the point is raised that the man who took 19 for 90 at Old Trafford in 1956 played for Surrey and not Yorkshire – is that he was a batsman who bowled a bit of medium-pace. If the off-spinner who could bat a bit had gone to Headingley in 1938 rather than Surrey in 1946 it would almost certainly have been a different story on both counts. Amongst those against whom he was competing in 1938 were Willie Watson, that elegant left-hander who played for Yorkshire until 1956, and then had four years as Leicestershire's captain as well as playing in 23 Tests for England; and Harry Halliday, a schoolboy prodigy at that time who played for the first team at 18 and went on to be Len Hutton's post-war opening partner. Also around were Vic Wilson, the East Riding farmer who skippered Yorkshire later to two Championship titles in three years; Ken Fiddling, a wicketkeeper-batsman who joined Northamptonshire after the war and Johnny Lawrence who never actually played for Yorkshire (he was a Somerset player from 1946 to 1955) but is destined to be forever remembered as the man who coached Geoffrey Boycott in his schoolboy years.

Jim was realistic enough to accept that while every Yorkshire-born boy in his day asked no more of life than to be chosen by his county, the odds against it happening even in purely arithmetical terms were very long indeed. Nevertheless, the very realisation that Yorkshire had shown no great interest in him in 1938 now reinforced his doubts when Surrey approached him in 1946. There were also the lingering thoughts about that steady job and regular wage. On leaving school as a bright, above-average student, he had got his first job in the local branch of the

Union Bank of Manchester, soon to be absorbed by Barclays. After being released at long last from the Army his first thoughts, naturally, were about steady, safe employment and reasoning that his mother's death had left him with no real incentive to return to his home county he got a transfer to a Barclays branch in London. With an eye to the future he sat a series of banking examinations, but he yearned for more cricket than simply one game a week, and so he accepted the Surrey offer of a trial – which in fact came as a surprise to him, as did the subsequent offer of a contract at £6 a week for the winter months plus match-fees in summer. He also had at this time the bait of a commission if he would sign on in the regular Army but that life did not appeal and so he resigned from the bank, declined the Army's offer with thanks – it's fascinating to speculate upon what sort of officer he would have made! – and became a full-time professional cricketer on his demobilisation in August, 1946.

Now in the years that followed and the Laker success-story developed, something like a conspiracy of silence was evident in official Yorkshire cricket circles about how this particular cricketer slipped through the net. He always talked like a Yorkshireman and his attitude to the game was very Yorkshire indeed. How was it then, people began to ask, that he played for Surrey? The official line was not that he had failed to impress as a colt but simply that he had gone to live in the south after demobilisation and so, if he had improved, it was not possible to monitor his progress. But is this strictly true? Can it be possible that with a wealth of evidence of Laker's ability being printed in the Bradford, Leeds and Shipley newspapers during 1944 and 1945 it had all escaped the notice of county officials and coaches?

Hidden away in the family scrapbooks can be found quite damning evidence that the talent-spotting system slipped up badly. Shortly after Laker's return from overseas service this paragraph appeared in the *Yorkshire Evening Post*:

> Knowing how close is Yorkshire's net, I don't suppose the Headingley intelligence service is unaware of the fact that Jim Laker, the Saltaire all-rounder, is home from overseas service.
>
> Laker, who is 23, may be the answer to the county's prayer for a class off-break bowler. He can bring his arm over high, can keep a length all day and on the word of South Africa's Dudley Nourse is an England player in the making.

Laker's name was also on a list of 35 colts due to be 'checked' by the coach, Arthur ('Ticker') Mitchell during the winter of 1945–46. Someone, somewhere failed to link that newspaper article with the fact that the young ex-serviceman did not attend that vetting session but seemed content to play club cricket 200 miles away in the London area. He wasn't the first, or the last, Yorkshireman to slip through the net, of course, but he was undoubtedly the most important one that got away. Thus, with hindsight, it seems to have been an act of folly when Yorkshire offered no objection to Surrey's registration of Laker and as he later told his friend and *Daily Express* associate Pat Gibson with a broad grin, 'It must have come as a terrible shock to them when I first went back to Bradford to play *against* them and they discovered that the modest, medium-paced trundler had changed into a genuine, round-the-wicket off-spinner.' Worse was to come, of course, when on that same Park Avenue ground he took eight wickets for two runs in the Test Trial. After his first season with Surrey, the county's annual report recorded, 'the success of D. G. W. Fletcher and J. C. Laker was most encouraging and the latter is to be congratulated on having been included in the MCC team that has toured the West Indies'. For the county in 1947, Laker took 71 wickets at 17.43 and scored 396 runs (avge 19.80) with a top score of 60. Despite all his doubts and fears he had made the grade in his first season, with an MCC tour as the icing on the cake. In Yorkshire, the Committee pondered on just how he had slipped through the net but there was nothing they could do about it now.

Fate, and the boredom of immediate post-war service in the Army, decreed that Jim Laker had to be a Surrey and not a Yorkshire cricketer. Yet Jim always felt that Yorkshire resented the way he had eluded them because he experienced an 'air of tension' when he returned to the broad acres to play. He went into the Headingley Committee room on occasions, when invited by personal friends, but he believed it strange that he had never had an official invitation, especially in the years when he was commentating on Test Matches. In this, I thought he was mistaken so I consulted Norman Yardley, former captain of Yorkshire and England, Committeeman, then President of the county: 'I always thought Jim had a bit of a chip on his shoulder about this,' said Norman. 'The policy at Test Matches is that the only official guests are past captains. I am sure there was no feeling of unease amongst our Committee — it wasn't as if Yorkshire had had any contretemps with Jim. I'm sure that when he was invited into the Committee room by a friend he would have been made most welcome.' A pause and then a majestically one-Yorkshireman-to-another rider: 'Come to think of it, I've never been invited officially into the Committee room at The Oval.'

I think Norman Yardley is right in believing that Jim had some sort of chip on his shoulder about Yorkshire, born of a kind of schizophrenic approach to the fact that he played for Surrey. He was in character and temperament, quintessentially a Yorkshireman. He had no great regard for authority and in particular he did not very much like amateurs or committees which, in part, explains why he publicly supported the Boycott cause in that player's bitter and prolonged battle with the Yorkshire Committee. I found this staggering. Not for one second would I (or did I) quarrel with a great player's assessment of another one. Indeed, that has never been the problem between the pro- and anti-Boycott factions. What I could never understand was Jim's championing the cause of a man who was so obviously at odds with so many of the men he actually played alongside. Jim had great qualities of loyalty; he must surely have seen that Boycott's main loyalty was to himself and a constant search for new personal records. I argued with him that if he had played for Yorkshire instead of Surrey his view of that dispute would have been different; he replied that it was exactly because he played for another county that he was able to take a more objective attitude – and possibly he was right to take that view. But it is a fact that while he was 100 per cent Surrey as a player, and, after the estrangement of the early 1960s, an energetic and conscientious Committeeman at The Oval, too, he thought and felt like a Yorkie all his life. It was the Yorkshireman who clashed with Freddie Brown and Peter May, the Yorkshireman who so despised Errol Holmes, his amateur captain in his early days with Surrey.

He shared with his more spectacular fellow-countryman, F. S. Trueman, the engaging habit of sauntering into the opposition's dressing-room before a first day's play and ostentatiously lining up potential victims. He knew the men who didn't like off-spin just as Fred knew the men who didn't like the ball whistling around their ears and each of them, in his individual fashion, was able to establish a psychological advantage before the players had even taken the field. Fred was known to mark a metaphorical cross in the middle of a batsman's forehead and stroll away with the cryptic comment, 'That's where I'm going to pin *theee*.' Jim, with the slow bowler's natural subtlety, contented himself with a throw-away line, 'Another catch for Lockie, there, I think.'

Yet with the match actually in progress he was as undemonstrative as Fred was volatile. He wore what Peter Walker (the Glamorgan all-rounder and specialist short-leg catcher) describes as 'an air of resigned indifference to his immediate fortunes' and yet everyone knew instinctively that to take this at face-value was to court disaster. Laker cared all right – and deeply too. He was remarkably adept as an *agent provocateur*, on the field and off it. He actively encouraged the unwary and unsuspecting *aficionado* to ask Tony Lock how the wickets were shared at Old Trafford in 1956, then stood back with a broad smile as Lock erupted. He delighted, at editorial meetings of *Wisden Cricket Monthly* (as David Frith, the Editor, recalls them) in waiting until a point when discussions had become desultory, then tossing in the bait-ball which resulted in two or three of his colleagues immediately going for the jugular while Jim sat back with a comfortable and intensely satisfied smile. If he wanted to reduce me to spluttering apoplexy he knew he had but to mention appreciatively the name of one who, in my view, had reached a position of eminence in the cricket-reporting world through outside influence rather than spending a year or two learning his trade. He really enjoyed, too, tossing out the suggestion that the Radio 3 commentary team were the poor relations of the cricket-broadcasting world but was quick to change the subject when the reply came swiftly, 'Why, then, do we get seven times more letters from the public than you and Richie and co.?' Oh yes. He was almost 100 per cent Yorkie, our Jim.

He might well have played for the county after all. In the early fifties an approach was made and he turned it down flat. Surrey had given him his chance and even though he understood Yorkshire's reasons for not signing him when they had the opportunity to do so, in cricketing terms he was a Surrey man and that is what he would remain. Even though Yorkshire then unearthed Bob Appleyard – a brilliant purveyor of off-spin among other varieties of bowling – Laker sauntered through the fifties as a member of a seven-times County Championship-winning side and it gave him perverse pleasure to see Yorkshire runners up twice and third on one occasion during those years.

LILLY

Lilly, petite and vivacious, escaped with her family from the Nazis in their native Austria in the late 1930s and found a home in Israel (then Palestine). As soon as foreign nationals were allowed to join the British services she enlisted in the A.T.S. and was posted to an ordnance depot in Egypt where Corporal Laker, J. C., was serving. It was not a case of love at first sight by any means; in fact it would be something like eight years before they married and Lilly remembers only one 'date' during the time they served in the same unit: 'We went to an absolute dive because I thought Jim hadn't enough money to go anywhere better. As it happened, I was wrong,' she added thoughtfully. Clearly Yorkshire principles of counting the pennies applied at that earliest stage of a relationship which was later to develop into a close, and very happy marriage. But the big N.C.O. at least made one lasting impression: 'I don't think he was a very good soldier. Being a Yorkshireman he was naturally a bit of a rebel and didn't like being told what to do.'

It was at a unit re-union in London that they met again after the war, by which time Lilly was working at Fulham Palace ('I believe Jim thought it was the Fulham *Palais* when I told him about it') for the Bishop of London. She had started as a clerk-typist, then developed her repertoire by taking a course in shorthand and when the accountant died she kept the books as well – a useful sort of lady to have around. Jim took a note of her phone number, musing, 'I go to Alf Gover's cricket school, which is quite close. We might have lunch together.' In the event, it was almost a year before he phoned and Lilly reflected philosophically that 'at least he had remembered the number'! They had lunch at the Star and Garter, on Putney Bridge – 'and he did nothing but talk about the girls in the West Indies'. But this time they stayed in touch. Jim went on the Commonwealth tour to India and they wrote regularly to each other. On 27 March, 1951, they were married.

They went on honeymoon by train to Bournemouth with the bride-groom making strenuous efforts to conceal their newly-wed status. 'When we changed at the hotel,' Lilly recalls, 'confetti fell out of our clothing and Jim spent ages picking up every piece from the floor. He insisted that we should walk down separately to dinner and when a man said to him, "Isn't it awful – all these newly-married couples in the place?" Jim agreed with him! And the London papers (the *Star*, *Evening News* and *Evening Standard*) were on sale in the hotel with our wedding pictures in all of them. It was ridiculous.' In the best honeymoon tradition it rained for five days!

It was a good marriage, which brought great happiness to them during the next 35 years. One of its best features was that Jim was always able to keep his public life quite separate from that with the family to whom he was endearingly devoted and, equally, Lilly never sought to intrude into his professional work. If her husband wanted her to be with him she was always available; if she wanted to do something of special interest or importance to her, Jim accompanied her if it was at all possible. He referred to Lilly as 'my mate' and the *double entendre* was probably not accidental because that is how their friends saw them – as mates, friends, good companions as well as husband, wife and parents. I have known many cricket wives and none more devoted than Lilly Laker. Jim, a no-nonsense and occasionally irascible companion in his man's world, was a different character within his own home environment. He adored the five grandchildren their daughters, Fiona and Angela, gave them (a sixth was born after Jim's death) and never regretted that he did not have a son. He knew only too well the burdens imposed on the male descendants of famous sportsmen and was content that his record would never be an albatross round the neck of a son. This did not prevent his taking immense delight and pride in the burgeoning talent of the eldest of their four grandsons, Jamie, however.

Lilly was not a cricket wife in the sense that she understood the game well or even enjoyed it but she did enjoy the friendships of other wives who were close to the game and, indeed, the ambience of cricket. She was loyal enough to 'hate it' if she heard, or read, that Jim hadn't bowled well, but she still regarded her first visit to a Test Match with a sort of dread in case she was expected to talk about the game with any degree of learning. Those fears proved to be unfounded when Dorothy Hutton and Barbara Watson took her under their wing and the only cause for concern she remembers from that first visit to Headingley was that ladies in the pavilion were required to wear hats! In fact she enjoyed that occasion – but not so much as going 'home' to Saltaire with Jim (they stayed with his sister in Baildon for the Test) and playing childish games which took him back to his boyhood, like retracing the steps from his home to his school – a sentimental little journey which may surprise those who knew Jim Laker only superficially, or perhaps simply as a cricketer. Not too many of them would say 'sentimental' is the first adjective which comes to mind.

The following winter (1951–52) Jim and Lilly undertook their first overseas trip together when a coaching engagement with the University club in Auckland took them to New Zealand. A 32-day voyage via Panama in the SS Rangitata was some compensation for a honeymoon in the rain in Bournemouth. They stayed with the parents of Don Taylor (with whom Jim had played service cricket in Egypt and Italy and who came over to play for Warwickshire between 1949 and 1953) and Jim played Plunkett Shield cricket for Auckland while Lilly worked in an insurance office. It was a good winter for them and they would have returned the following year but for Lilly's pregnancy and Jim's insistence that the child should be born in England. But before returning home in 1952 they enjoyed a tour of Australia which served to make Jim, at least, all the keener to see more of the country, preferably as a cricket tourist.

To many of us, Jim Laker was a tough, rugged character who could well take care of himself, who needed no help when it came to his tussles with authority, whether it was at The Oval or in the wider sphere of Test cricket. He was known never to suffer fools gladly; he had firm, and sometimes fixed, views on players and policies, pitches and principles; he could alienate as well as attract. His family, naturally enough, saw another and more important side of Jim. They were saddened by his distress at what he saw as the break-up of a wonderful team-spirit in Surrey in 1959. The immediate cause of his retirement in 1959 might well have been the condition of his overworked spinning finger but it cannot be totally dissociated from the atmosphere of uneasy truce which had existed between him and Peter May during the past year and a bewildered feeling of disillusionment with the England selectors. Amongst his family and a select circle of friends he could find refuge from all that and their love and loyalty were invaluable. When, in 1967, he was rehabilitated by MCC they rejoiced with him as they did when the breach with Surrey had been healed and he was made an honorary life member of the county club. He joined Surrey's public relations committee and then became cricket chairman though he later confessed that he might not have taken that job had not Mickey Stewart been the cricket manager. The Stewarts were part of that close circle of intimate family friends.

A warm friendship had developed between Jim and Mickey shortly after the future England cricket manager had completed his National Service and taken part in Surrey's pre-season two-day match. In some ways it was a case of unlike poles attracting, as Stewart recalls:

> I was, perhaps, the embodiment of physical enthusiasm in that I liked to run around, dive around, generally be a busy sort of cricketer. Jim was a person who had schooled himself, I believe, to move at a more

sedate pace, to sort things out. It was reflected in terms of personality: Jim took a more balanced view of things whereas as a young man I was apt to jump to conclusions. The fact that he took a liking to me was ultimately of immense benefit to me and I think he played a big part in my development, very much to my advantage. Also he was the type of man who, if he felt his help was appreciated, could be very forthcoming. On the other hand, and quite naturally, he only had to get the faintest scent that his advice was not welcome and that was very definitely the end of that.

Between the two men there was another basis for personal friendship – association football. Jim would talk about his boyhood days watching Bradford City and his own involvement in the game as an amateur player; Mickey was a talented footballer and his performances with Corinthian Casuals were watched, from time to time, by Jim. When Stewart married, the sporting association developed into a family friendship between he and his wife Sheila and Jim and Lilly. It was an association which both couples prized highly.

The privacy of the Lakers' family life was precious to them but it had to be surrendered, at least temporarily, when events at Old Trafford in 1956 made Jim the most talked-about sportsman in the world. The girls were photographed almost as much as their father, which they probably enjoyed, but when the time came for Mother to reveal all about 'That Man Laker' as the *Sunday Graphic* headlined their exclusive feature, Lilly shuddered in horror at the prospect. And the interviewer no doubt shuddered in horror, too, when her reply to the first question was:

I am sorry if this is going to disappoint you but he's just an ordinary man in everything he does. He has no fads about food and no particular hobbies. He doesn't like coming shopping with me. He can't – or won't – cook but he's a generous man with money. Sounds just like any other husband, doesn't he?

The impish sense of humour indicated in those last eight words was obviously a help in steering Lilly through the inevitable loneliness of a cricketing-widow in days when fewer opportunities presented themselves from spending much time with her husband. This was because: (1) accompanying players on tour was severely discouraged by MCC and (2) professional cricketers of the 1940s and 50s were simply not well-paid enough to be able to afford it. She told the *Sunday Graphic*:

Jim is often away for 10 or 12 days in a row and sometimes, when he goes on a winter tour, it can be as much as seven months. Even when he is playing at home he can be out four evenings a week — and for a cricketer's wife there are no such things as week-ends. To make a marriage like ours succeed, I have come to realise that a wife must have tolerance and a sense of humour. Having your husband in the limelight all the time calls for a lot more hard work than most marriages.

That, of course, is absolutely right and it was even more applicable 30 and 40 years ago. Modern players are infinitely more affluent than they were in Laker's day and player-power has grown to an extent which would lead to a sort of revolution if wives were not allowed to join their husbands in the pleasant climes of Australia, New Zealand and some parts of the West Indies. I have even known them to arrive in India for Christmas, or towards the end of a longish tour — though the handful who chose to join the tourists in Kanpur in the closing days of the 1981– 82 tour were more than slightly disillusioned by the quality of their accommodation!

Wives of Lilly's era had to endure months of separation and to bring up the children alone because, quite simply, there was no alternative. The story of first-class cricket in the fifties and sixties is, sadly, littered with examples of broken marriages and it is quite true that it took a special sort of relationship to withstand the pressures. I was made aware of this in a very personal way when England were away in the West Indies in early 1960. Brian Statham's son became seriously ill while his father was 3,500 miles away and I saw something of the anguish of our Manchester neighbour's wife, Audrey, until Brian flew home to be with her and their son.

This sort of situation can lead to acts of kindness and consideration such as one Lilly remembers from another West Indian tour, that of 1953–54. Jim retired hurt after being hit by a bouncer from Frank King in Trinidad and Lilly knew nothing of this until her phone rang just before 10 o'clock one night. The call came from my friend and colleague, Brian Johnston, covering the tour for the BBC and it was absolutely typical of the man. 'Don't let me frighten you,' he told Lilly, 'but you'll be hearing something about Jim on the 10 o'clock news. I wanted you to know that it is not as bad as it sounds.' And the news, of course, carried Brian's report of the day's play which included Jim's injury. Jim's personal recollection of the incident, recalled with dry humour, appears elsewhere in this story.

Lilly's own story of a wifely sympathy for a cricketing husband is one which I have always found quite delightful. Jim came home from a day's play at The Oval in 1954 and mentioned that he had 'got 113 today'. Thinking that he meant no wicket for 113 runs, Lilly decided that quiet commiseration was called for and maintained a reverent silence. Only next day, when she read her morning paper, did she realise that J.C. had made a career-best score of 113.

THE
BIGGEST
SNOB

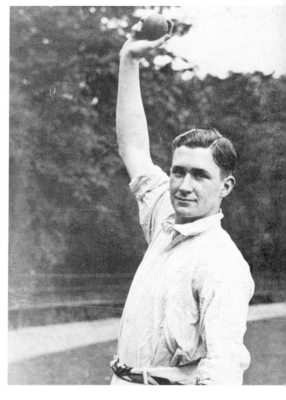

ABOVE How angelic can you look…at 13? Choirboy Jim in 1936

RIGHT Jim as a schoolboy cricketer. Hadn't 'Persil' been invented by then?

BELOW The prefects at Salts High School. Jim centre, back row

The schoolboy footballer – Front row, second from right

Salts High School cricket team, 1937. Jim fifth from left, back row

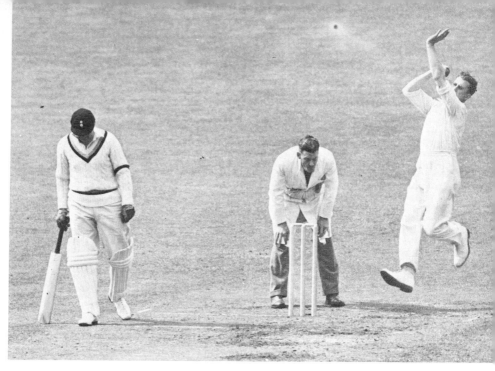

The easy lope to the wicket, then the high, right-over-the-top delivery. Jim in action against Derbyshire, 1949 *(Keystone)*

It's turning, Jim, round the wicket against South Africa, 1951 – only 6 for 55 that day *(Keystone)*

Jim and Lilly set off for their trip to New Zealand in the winter of 1951-52 *(Topham)*

Meeting H.M. The Queen at Lord's during the Second Test against India, 1952 *(Sport & General)*

Off to the West Indies in 1953, but not on a banana boat this time.
Left rank, top to bottom: Tom Graveney, Ken Suttle, Reg Spooner,
Willie Watson, Trevor Bailey, Charles Palmer (manager), Len Hutton
(captain). Right rank: Jim Laker, Tony Lock, Peter May, Brian Statham,
Freddie Trueman, Johnny Wardle, Alan Moss, Godfrey Evans, Denis
Compton *(Topham)*

The natural twins, Eric and Alec Bedser, greet Jim on his return from the West Indies, 1954 *(Topham)*

The ideal way to relax – at Wimbledon Golf Club *(Sport & General)*

Caught Laker, bowled Lock, for a change. Surrey v Somerset in 1955
(Central Press)

Dinner together for the England and Australian teams at The Oval,
1953. Captains Len Hutton and Lindsay Hassett cut the cake
(Central Press)

'This is how it was done'. A week after his 19 for 90 at Old Trafford, Jim Laker shows how he spins the ball to schoolboys at the Children's Exhibition at Olympia. Brian Statham looks on and reflects that it's easier than fast bowling *(Keystone)*

One footballer salutes another – Jim with Stanley Matthews (centre) who is celebrating 25 years in League football. *(Sport & General)*

Jim had very strong feelings indeed on matters like class distinction. I never discussed with him his attitude to officers during his Army career – no doubt a sixth sense urged that it would prove a fruitless debate – though I wondered once or twice how he would have fared in a fighting unit where discipline was stricter than that he encountered in the R.A.O.C. It is difficult to avoid the feeling that he might have spent more time in the glasshouse than on the cricket field and so we have to be grateful that he did indeed settle for ordnance matters. Cricket might otherwise have lost one of its finest practitioners. We have the view of his lady wife that he 'didn't like being told what to do' and he was not long into his professional career before he was on something of a collision course with an amateur captain – 'Errol Reginald Thorold Holmes was my first captain at Surrey and quite frankly he was the biggest snob I ever met.'

Holmes (Malvern and Oxford) played in a Harlequin cap and that, for starters, was the proverbial red rag to a bull, especially when the bull was of the north country professional type and while he was a fine player of fast or fast-medium bowling on good pitches, he was not so resourceful against off-spinners. Early encounters in the Surrey nets between Laker and his captain did not enhance feelings of cordiality between the two of them. The situation was exacerbated by Surrey's strict adherence to the amateur–professional distinction in travel and accommodation. While the amateurs took taxis to the railway station the pros (in London) would travel by underground. At St Pancras (or Paddington, etc.) the amateurs went to their first-class compartment, the pros into third class. On arrival at the town of destination, the amateurs would be driven to the best hotel while the pros walked to their more modest pub. Allowances for a three-day game amounted to no more than £4 for dinner, bed and breakfast, which would have been adequate in 1947 but little more than that. And really the only time the two factions got together during a game was on the field of play.

For men like Errol Holmes, who had played before the war, this was no more and no less than the natural order of things, and to be realistic, it was not unacceptable to the older professionals in the side like Alf Gover, Tom Barling, Bob Gregory and Stan Squires. But it was alien to the new generation of post-war pros like Jim Laker. Had not the returning servicemen been largely responsible for voting out the immortal Winston Churchill and the Tories, substituting the egalitarianism of a Labour

Government? If Laker's post-war employment had not involved the game of cricket to which he was so deeply devoted, clearly it would not have lasted very long. (Almost paradoxically, he was a member of the Conservative Party and always voted Tory.)

Salvation – at least for Laker's peace of mind – came in the burly form of Stuart Surridge, an amateur fast-medium bowler who had joined Surrey in 1947, Jim's first full season in the game, and had played with him in both first and second elevens. He was appointed captain in 1952 and led Surrey to five successive county championships. Here was a man very much to Jim Laker's liking:

> He will go down in the record books as a fairly ordinary cricketer, though in fairness his performances were always a little bit better than he was given credit for. If you look back, he took around 500 wickets in his career [506 in fact] and he managed to hang on to about 50 catches at short-leg every season. So you could not really label him a passenger. But it was as a captain, a leader of men, that he was one of the most dynamic characters ever to set foot on a cricket field. He did not believe it was possible for Surrey to lose a match. As a result, he made a few mistakes, but not very many. He was also the greatest retriever of lost causes I have ever known. And he had the happy inborn knack of knowing how to handle individuals. One has to remember that that side, which eventually contained 10 Test cricketers, included some very different temperaments and personalities. All in all, he was a very popular guy, *even in the professionals' dressing room.*

The italics are the author's own because the last half-dozen words will be seen by all who knew Jim as an indication of his reluctance to abandon his prejudice! Surridge, in fact, took his style of captaincy from Brian Sellers, another cricketer of relatively modest pretensions, who nevertheless handled a team of grizzled Yorkshire stars firmly through the 1930s, when the side won seven out of nine championships. Surridge remembers playing in a game against Yorkshire at The Oval just after the war when Surrey looked like winning. 'All of a sudden, he turned the game round,' says Surridge, grimacing at the memory. 'I think I had been last out and I was cursing to myself as we left the field. He said, "What's the matter with thee, lad?" I replied, "We were going to win this game when you turned it round on us," and he said, "Always remember this, lad – it's no bloody good being second." All I could reply was, "You might live to regret that one day?"' Glamorgan players of that era, and the next decade, might well claim that Wilf Wooller had many of the qualities of both Sellers and Surridge, though he never had the same resources of man-power.

In common with most counties, Surrey had resumed after the war with a nucleus of seasoned players and a leavening of new ones. After a few years it was time for the old guard to change and while Squires, Barling and Gregory had gone they had been replaced by Tom Clark, Bernie Constable and David Fletcher; the Bedser twins were established, as was Laker himself; Tony Lock had developed into an accomplished slow left-armer and Peter Loader had come from the Beddington Club to share the new ball with Alec Bedser, while Peter May promised to be the finest batsman in the country. Surridge had the firepower and the batting strength to compare with Yorkshire's all-round talent of the time − Hutton, Watson, Wilson, Lester, Close, Trueman, Appleyard, Wardle − and these were the two most powerful sides throughout the 1950s. But it was Surrey who won seven consecutive county championships in all.

As early as their first second-eleven match together, Surridge noticed that Laker had 'something about him'. He was very much a northerner, surly in some ways, but he wanted to win. 'That was the first thing I marked,' recalls Surridge. 'He always wanted to win.' One of the earliest conversations he remembers was one in which Jim insisted, 'If you want to be a spin bowler you have first got to learn to spin the ball. It's no use bowling line and length if you are not spinning it.'

Now this philosophy might perhaps be at variance with that of some of his distinguished fellow-Yorkshiremen, at least those of the old school, but Laker had, of course, brought about his own transition from seam to spin bowling by spending long hours in practising and perfecting his ability to turn the ball, and there is no doubt that he did become a most formidable *spinner* of it unlike, perhaps, some of today's slow bowlers who are content with a mere run-restricting line and length. Just about everyone who played alongside or against him very quickly testifies to hearing the formidable 'whirring' of the ball through the air after an audible snap of the fingers as it left his hand. Laker was not above creating his own illusions, either. He developed an ability to click the fingers of his left hand in a way which reproduced the sound of the ball leaving his spinning hand so that if he found himself on an unresponsive wicket he could create the impression that he was still giving it a tremendous 'flick' and so have the batsman playing for something which was not always happening.

His partnership with Lock was of course legendary and it was, naturally, a tremendous advantage to their captain that there was such a fierce rivalry between the two. If one had an outstanding first-innings performance it made the other all the more determined to top it in the second. They were as utterly different in style and temperament as they were in the use of a bowling arm. Surridge chuckles at the memory:

If you wanted Tony to go you had to give him a few swear-words now and again. (And, incidentally, I'd like to make the point that we never swore at the opposition and certainly never at the umpires. But we did swear a bit amongst ourselves). But with Jim, one swear-word and he was finished. I swore at him only once and he couldn't bowl for an hour. Couldn't bowl. Had no idea what was going on. With Jim, you had to encourage him – 'Come on, Jim. Get it going.' He wasn't so much angry that I had sworn as upset, deeply upset. He just couldn't stand that sort of approach at all.

Perhaps the most remarkable revelation to emerge from a long conversation with Stuart Surridge was that when Jim took all 10 Australian wickets for 88 for Surrey at The Oval in 1956, 'he only really turned one ball'. And just how did that come about?

Well, it was a beautiful wicket. Simply, he kidded them. He could do it all – off the pitch, through the air. He could turn it when he wanted to. But he could do it all, you see. When I look at spin bowlers today I don't see calluses or corns on their spinning fingers, but Tony and Jim, you know, the only time when they were out of the side, probably for one game or something like that, was when they had to nurse their fingers because the corns had been ripped open. I might mention that some people used to talk a load of rubbish about The Oval wickets. I never asked the groundsman to produce a particular kind of wicket; we played on what he produced and I think you'll find the seamers actually took more wickets than Laker and Lock.

Another aspect of the Laker–Lock partnership was that each of them was a specialist catcher off the other's bowling – Lock the incomparable short-leg, Laker useful in the gulley. Skipper Surridge had already served in a side where there was laughter when a catch went down and he didn't like that at all. When he took command he resolved that catching was going to play a very important part in his plan of campaign and a list of specialist close-catchers was drawn up. Laker was afterwards to say that Lock was of greater help to him than he was to Tony and indeed the sandy-haired left-armer developed catching behind the wicket on the leg-side into an extremely aggressive art form but Laker, in his first-class career, held 271 catches of which a high proportion were from Lock's bowling. The exact figure does not appear in any reference book that I have seen but I would certainly not bet against someone, somewhere, having it neatly entered in his own private store of statistics. (I have an extremely healthy respect for the statistician's role. During a Test between New Zealand and West Indies in Wellington in 1987, Vivian Richards delayed taking the new ball until 177 overs had been bowled with the old one, which by then had the density of a feather duster. I idly mused, in commentary, on whether this might be a record but supposed that no one had collected *that* particular piece of information. Within half-an-hour a call had been received at Radio New Zealand headquarters and relayed to us at the ground. It *was* a record; the previous highest number of overs with one ball was 172 – by the West Indies on their previous tour of New Zealand!) Lock's total of first-class catches was 830, so clearly Jim's tribute to his partner is deserved, yet it is fascinating to look at old Surrey scorecards and note the number of times 'c Lock b Laker' is echoed by 'c Laker b Lock'. They will be forever thought of as a brilliant bowling pair but their catching partnership is worth researching, too.

Returning for a moment to Stuart Surridge's memories of Laker, a boundless admiration has to be recorded:

> He had the most marvellous command of length without ever neglecting to spin the ball. I fielded at short-leg to him for years and I never got hit, not once. He just did not give the batsman a chance to hit me ... it really was quite remarkable. He was *great*, there is no doubt about it.

Why, then, did Laker not play in more Tests? The answer to that one is more difficult and Surridge does not have the answer. Neither, however, does anyone else. And it is undoubtedly true that Surridge was closer to Laker as a captain than anyone else in his career. The reason for that, Surridge thought, was 'probably due to my father':

> He made me start at the bottom in the family (sports equipment) business by simply becoming one of the work-force. I lived with the chaps in their little cottages and I worked alongside them so that – bearing in mind some of the amateur captains of that period and their backgrounds – perhaps I was able to understand the professional players a little bit better when I captained Surrey. Certainly I positioned

myself at short-leg because I wasn't going to ask anyone to field in a position I wouldn't occupy myself. My reflexes were good and I thought I could do the job when we set out to find our specialists but that was only part of it. It's obviously true that other people had their problems with Jim, but I never did.

If you press me for a reason for this I suppose I've got to go back to the time when I learned that all men are different in some ways. They have different feelings and sensitivities, react differently in some situations. In that Surrey side we had a collection of quite different personalities and they all had to be handled differently. Alec [Bedser] was marvellous, of course. You just gave him the ball and said 'bowl' and he never wanted to come off, but Peter Loader was as different from Alec as chalk and cheese – a bit like Jim and Lockie. One morning he didn't want to bowl, tried to take himself off, and as Alec was bowling from the other end the ball went to Loader who *kicked* it back towards Alec. I made him go and pick it up and throw it to the bowler in the proper manner. And I kept him bowling for most of the morning.

After a reflective pause, Surridge then chuckled, 'He bowled bloody well, too.'

Jim Laker wrote three books about his life and one of the very few people to appear in their pages with unqualified approval is Stuart Surridge. A glance at some of the names of those Jim observed with less wholehearted admiration indicates the depths of the Surridge–Laker mutual admiration society:

Peter May As an England captain, aloof and distant, appearing not to like mixing with his team; had a fear of the press – afraid to do or say anything which might leave itself open to misinterpretation.

Colin Cowdrey As a captain, does silly things which no Test captain can afford. He has said and written often enough that he disapproves of the 'hard' captaincy practised by Hutton and May, that he likes to think of cricket as a jolly game and to play it in that spirit. This is all very well but it doesn't work in Test matches.

Len Hutton I sometimes used to wonder why I was in a side under Hutton; I know he didn't dislike me personally, though you might have thought so. His qualities as a captain were diminished by his obsession for the fast bowlers. However, Hutton has made a success of his life in cricket and I begrudge him nothing. He had his successes and failures – and probably deserved both.

Freddie Brown (Manager in Australia, 1958–59) Soon, and without regret, I was out of his uncomfortable jurisdiction and on my way home.

Johnny Wardle Wardle was a selfish player who gave an immense amount of trouble to a captain [Ronnie Burnet] who was, beyond doubt, doing his best and who was therefore entitled to expect every support from his senior professional. The popular idea of Wardle the comic is not strictly true and his is a temperament and personality that many people have found it hard to like.

In listing those critical comments, let me say at once that they are by no means the whole story. Jim rarely criticised without a leavening of approval; he just did not find something disapproving to say and leave it at that. But I have taken those comments out of strict context and listed them to indicate that when Jim indulged in *wholehearted* approval, without listing a weakness or a shortcoming, it meant he was talking or writing about a person he regarded as rather special. And so we see:

When I first came into the Surrey side, bowling to three short-legs who stood about twice as far from the bat as they should have done and who were, anyway, strictly in the non-bending class – under Stuart Surridge's captaincy all that changed ... under Surridge we were a keen side, a good one, and no less sporting than the next. We played cricket as it should be played. Idealism is all very well in its place: some people wrinkle their noses at the expression 'playing to win'. All right cricket at its best is played for pleasure but where's the man who doesn't get more pleasure from winning than losing?

Considering Jim's deep-seated aversion to amateur players ('The removal of the distinction between the gentlemen and the players remains the best thing that has happened in my lifetime' – J. C. Laker, 1985), his relationship with Surridge was probably one of the happiest associations in his playing life. From Jim's extensive repertoire of anecdotes I single out one which illustrates the sort of half-incredulous, half-affectionate regard with which Surrey regarded their captain in the mid-fifties:

Surrey v Worcestershire at The Oval in 1954. Play did not start until two o'clock because of overnight rain and Stuart put Worcestershire in to bat on a wet wicket (uncovered pitches in those days). Locky and I bowled them out for 25 with their last seven wickets falling for just five runs. An hour before the close we had reached 92 for three with Peter May going well on 31, the wicket apparently easing and most of us sitting on the balcony with our boots off and our feet up. Suddenly we heard our idiot of a captain on the amateurs' balcony upstairs clapping his hands to declare and a few minutes later Surridge was marching into our dressing-room to find it in a state of panic with people hurriedly getting dressed or searching for boots.

I will always remember Alec Bedser looking at him and saying, 'Skipper, you've got to remember that someone else can play this game as well as us,' to which Stuart replied, 'Nonsense. We've got enough. We'll bowl 'em out again.' Out we went again to take two more wickets that night and inside an hour next morning we had claimed the remaining eight. Amazingly, we had won by an innings in under a day's play. We were sitting in the dressing-room reflecting on it all when Stuart came bursting in, shouting, 'Well done, well done.' Again Alec Bedser looked at him and said, 'You are a golden boy, a lucky so-and-so, you really are.' Again Stuart had an answer: 'Well, you might say that but I did ring the Met Office before I declared and the forecast was diabolical.' And sure enough, the rain started pouring shortly afterwards; if we had not got it over so quickly we would never have finished the game.

I like the story particularly because it not only illustrates quite graphically the differing attitudes of seasoned professionals and the amateur with flair but it gives us a taste of the dressing-room atmosphere of a successful side which is buoyant, confident and pulling together. It is an atmosphere which I have not quite found anywhere else in sport.

Trevor Bailey was another amateur player of Jim's day who figured high on the 'approved' list, possibly because he didn't really regard Trevor as an amateur (he was secretary of Essex as well as a player), but he had a tremendous professional respect for Trevor:

Bailey is that rarest thing in cricket — a real all-rounder. Bailey is the nearest to the real thing I know. He isn't a *great* player, of course, because he lacks the 'spark', but he has a great temperament. We joke about Bailey and some have had hard words to say about him but there is no denying he has done very well for English cricket. No player did more to bring the Ashes back in 1953, which is worth remembering when Trevor is, as often, in the critical firing line. He is, what's more, an excellent tourist, a good mixer and the finest maker of champagne cocktails in the business.

Now after 20 years or so of personal association – respectful on my part because he is a brilliant, if occasionally controversial, expert comments man for Radio 3's Test Match Special – those words delight me. T. E. Bailey is a good friend and excellent colleague in cricket broadcasting and I have always loved the stories of occasions when he drove the Australians into a frenzy of frustration.

Laker was a ringside spectator for one of them – at Headingley, in 1953, and he told the story with huge glee:

> The position at the start of the [last] day was that we were 75 runs on with five wickets left and in trouble. Several players were injured and before play started Compton had a pain-killing injection for his damaged hand. While this was taking effect, Evans came and went and I joined Bailey, whose score was moving on with the speed of a tired hedgehog. At 1.27 p.m. an over finished; Bailey and I had put on 55 of which he had scored just seven! The Australians were crossing for the last over before lunch when Bailey beckoned me. We met in the middle of the wicket. 'It's a lovely day,' remarked Trevor, looking up into the bright, blue sky, 'and we haven't a chance of an appeal against the light. But I can't say that I feel like another over before lunch ...' He appealed. And the Aussies, knowing that the umpire's consultation would take too long for another over to start, walked resignedly in.
>
> After lunch, Keith Miller gave Bailey the full treatment – bouncers, yorkers, everything. He almost went berserk when, after bowling one bumper and preparing for another thunderbolt, he had to stop almost in his delivery-stride as Bailey stepped away from the wicket and, with a bored air, adjusted his glove.

Doesn't that just conjure up a picture of great Ashes cricket which is infinitely preferable to close-to-the-wicket 'sledging' of batsmen, to the petulant knocking out of stumps after dismissal, to arguing with umpires on the field and whingeing about them off it?

Bailey had a boundless admiration for Laker as a *thinking* spin bowler and has recently recalled (in *The Spinner's Web*, with Fred Trueman) a prime example of his artistry during Jim's short spell of 30 matches, 1962–64, as, amazingly, an amateur with Essex:

> He was playing for Essex in a county match of no particular importance on a dead track at Leicester. A novice left-hander came in to face J.C. and played the first three deliveries with an immaculate full forward

defensive. The fourth was given more air and just about straightened from round the wicket and was given the same treatment. The fifth was appreciably shorter, quicker, and went with the arm into the batsman who instinctively moved back and was lbw before he had even time to realise he had been set up. In the Leicestershire second innings, Jim repeated his own version of the 'sting' except on this occasion I was already appealing from short extra-cover before the ball had left the hand. Only a great bowler with perfect control could twice attempt and accomplish that bowling confidence trick.

Compared with spin bowling 30 and 40 years later, Laker's figures for Surrey make fascinating reading in themselves (see the statistical section at the back of this book for full details) as well as providing an illuminating comment on the way the game has changed.

From his first full season (1947) onwards, Laker was out of the top 10 of the first-class averages only three times: 1948, 1955 (when Fred Titmus in 10th position in the list, had 191 wickets at 16.31!) and 1959. Laker was sixth in the averages in 1947 and 1949, third in 1950, eighth in 1951 and 1952, ninth in 1953, sixth in 1954 and 1956, fourth in 1957 and sixth in 1958. And this immense success, this tremendous striking rate, was achieved in the face of very strong opposition – not only around the country but within his own side as well. It earned him just five lines in the *Surrey Yearbook* when he retired in 1959:

> At the end of the season, Laker, J. C., was not re-engaged at his own request. His outstanding ability as an off-spin bowler needs no emphasis and regret at his retirement from first-class cricket will be universal, particularly as this has been occasioned by wear and tear of his spinning finger. Our thanks are due to him for his great bowling for Surrey and England since 1947.

Peter Walker was an accomplished all-rounder who played 437 matches for Glamorgan and lists as the three main regrets of his cricketing life the fact that he never saw either Don Bradman or Wally Hammond play the game and he never fielded short-leg to Jim Laker. Walker was, in fact, one of the outstanding short-leg fieldsmen of his day, but his three Tests for England came in 1960, the year after Laker retired at Surrey, and he did not return to international cricket during his brief subsequent spell with Essex. Walker held 697 catches in his first-class career, 250 of them in the short-leg area from the bowling of Don Shepherd, whom he rated the best off-spinner never to play for England. So he is very much an expert witness in this look at the life and times of J. C. Laker. In fact Walker scored his maiden county hundred playing against Surrey (with Laker, Lock, Bedser and Loader in the opposition attack) at Swansea in 1958. As he recalls it, 'The century took me the best part of two days and as a short-leg myself, the most difficult part was trying to keep out Laker with Tony Lock about three feet away from my hip pocket.' The St Helens ground in those days was a renowned slow turner of a wicket and century-making was far from easy. Dismissing his innings with the distinctly over-modest description of 'a varied collection of snicks and mis-hit drives', Walker remembers with great clarity being impressed by the Laker attitude:

While the other three England bowlers were not reluctant to dish out a choice selection of verbal flak, Jim remained unmoved. He was the original cricketing sphinx. On the field he wore an air of resigned indifference to his immediate fortunes and yet, as I was to discover when our paths became more firmly entwined as fellow-commentators, he *did* care.

Tony Lock certainly knew that Jim cared when it would not be obvious from the spectators' seats:

I could never judge from Jim's action the speed at which he'd released the ball or how much or how little he had spun it. That's why I got into the habit of standing so close. I reckoned it was better to be within range of an edge than to be too deep. If one did fall short of me I made sure I didn't look at Jim. You could feel his disgust from a distance of 20 yards!

For this revelation I am indebted again to P. M. Walker for it occurred during a conversation he had with Tony Lock. It must have been a talk, between two of the greatest of short-leg fieldsmen, which one wishes had been recorded in full.

Yet another authority on short-leg fielding is Mickey Stewart, who found himself in the Laker leg trap almost as soon as he became established in the Surrey side, and spent five years there from 1954 until Jim's retirement.. He gives us a fascinating glimpse of Laker's 'caring' qualities. While others have recalled Laker's clear, if unspoken, disgust at a dropped catch from his bowling, Stewart shows us a completely different side of the man:

He was a bowler with tremendous control of everything – pace, loop, direction, length and spin – and he had an extremely shrewd, analytical brain which enabled him to read, expertly, what the batsman was trying to do. It was, in fact, easier to field there when I started than it is today because batsmen didn't whack the ball as hard. I started when people still played with their bat in front of the pad and the inside edge more often than not went to Lock, at *backward* short-leg; then they started bringing their bat back so it was more or less level with the pad and the catch went to me; now it's gone right back so that it's pad first, then bat, and the edge goes on the off side, hence the use of the silly point position. But very few people actually swept the ball in those first years when I fielded at short-leg to Jim. If the ball pitched off stump or on the line of the stumps at all, very few people tried to sweep. One of the few great exponents of the shot at that time was Ken Grieves, the Australian who played for Lancashire. He was a magnificent sweeper and Jim just wouldn't let me field there to Ken because he knew that the batsman would sweep, with the spin, no matter where he pitched the ball. I couldn't understand it because he was such a superb bowler. I was willing to stand there but Jim simply wouldn't have it. That was a side of him which too few people appreciated. He was a deeply caring and sensitive person in everything and he would have been distraught if I had been hit off his bowling. I remember once when I had to talk him into letting me stand in close and just in front – we were playing Hampshire at Portsmouth and Roy Marshall played a couple of magnificent innings. When Hampshire were following on I said to Jim, 'Let me get in there, in front. He'll probably think it's cheeky, try to hit me and he might knock it up to mid-on and get out.' Jim looked at me and said, 'You're bloody mad', but I did get my way and Roy did actually hole out.

Three years after his retirement from Surrey, and with the shockwaves of his criticisms in *Over to Me* still reverberating around the cricket world, Laker enjoyed a brief new playing career with Essex – 30 games over the seasons 1962/3/4. Just how this came about is interesting (and perhaps may never be fully explained) because the versions of the two people involved, Jim and Trevor Bailey, are profoundly, though light-heartedly, at odds.

The Laker version was this:

One night – or in the early hours of the morning to be more exact! – I found myself in deep conversation with Trevor Bailey. We were in Manchester with Denis Compton and Godfrey Evans in connection with some promotional work we were doing. But Trevor, as usual, was promoting Essex — and he must have been making a good job of it for the following morning I picked up the *Daily Express* and was shocked to discover that I had agreed to play for Essex as an amateur.

The Bailey version is somewhat different:

> I was speaking at a sporting dinner with him in Manchester and we travelled back together by train the following morning. Over a very good breakfast I casually mentioned that Essex were short of a spin bowler and was he interested in occasionally helping us? To my delight and surprise, Jim agreed to play a few games for my county as an amateur and we specially registered him.

Notwithstanding the contrasting recollections — whether it was early in the morning or even earlier, over breakfast, they had indeed had a good night and old friends such as those two never fall out over a matter of circumstantial detail — the repercussions were predictable, even though they surprised Bailey:

> Some of my Committee were not in favour. I found this hard to comprehend because I had acquired a great cricketer and a personality for nothing, not unlike a football manager persuading George Best, when he was reliable, to turn out for his club without wages. In contrast, the Essex players were without exception delighted to have the opportunity of playing alongside a master craftsman.

Jim, by this time sick of the controversy which had resulted from his book and deeply wounded by the withdrawal of his MCC and Surrey honorary membership, relied a great deal on Bailey's influence with his own Committee and this, allied to his personal regard for Trevor, persuaded him that he might well enjoy a limited number of matches free of professional pressures.

On the other hand, Bailey's admiration for Laker's bowling is evident from his comments elsewhere in these pages and in his own books. His high regard was justified from the moment Jim bowled his first delivery for Essex — though the memory is not shared with equal pleasure by everyone: 'He made his usual casual approach, over went his arm, the ball dropped on exactly the right spot, turned sufficiently to take the inside edge — and Gordon Barker, [himself a Yorkshire exile] put down the catch at backward short-leg.' Barker's anger at missing the catch was only transcended by his fury that the miss earned him bigger headlines than when he made a century!

Jim, it has to be remembered, was now 40 and playing a couple of matches, then having the next two off, presented its own problems: 'You stiffen up more easily in the forties and every time I returned to Essex it would take me at least one game to loosen up again.' But he left behind one of those celebrated one-liners for inclusion in the folklore of Essex cricket. After being asked for his advice on whether to bat or field by his captain he went out for a visit of inspection of a pitch which was – as so many Essex pitches were for so long – very green and took a strangely long time. When he finally returned, Trevor asked, 'Where have you been?' 'Trying to *find* the pitch,' was the reply.

Before joining Essex, and while developing a number of business interests, Jim returned for a season of league cricket – not in the Bradford League where the money in any case would not have been as high, but to Norton, in Staffordshire. He was paid £60 a match which was big money indeed in 1960 – just £15 less than his last Test Match fee had been, in fact – and there were additional rewards in the form of collections for five wickets or 50 runs. Despite the problems of bowling on relatively small grounds to batsmen who did not always show proper respect for what the ball might be doing, he did 'all right,' as he put it. That, in the eyes of Norton officials was an over-modest under-assessment of his season in the Potteries. They thought Jim Laker did a bit better than all right and to prove it they signed as his replacement Gary Sobers.

WHY
ONLY 46 TESTS?

In an age when England players have been known to play more than 60 Tests on the trot, when the country's leading off-spinner can go through a home series without taking a wicket and then be picked automatically for *three* winter series not only as a player but as vice-captain of the party, it seems little short of unbelievable that of the 94 Tests played during his time at the top, Jim Laker took part in less than half of them — 46 to be exact. And this at a time when he was widely regarded as very definitely the best off-spinner in the world.

In his first series (in the West Indies, 1947–48) he bowled more overs and took more wickets than anyone else and in his last, when he finally achieved his burning desire to tour Australia after twice being unaccountably passed over, he did the same. Yet during the intervening years it was a story of being in and out of the side in the most bewildering fashion. The full story reads like this:

1947–48 Debut at the Kensington Oval, Barbados	played in four Tests out of four
1948 at home to Australia	three out of five
1948–49 tour to South Africa	nil (did not tour)
1949 home to New Zealand	one out of four
1950 home to West Indies	one out of four
1950–51 tour to Australia and New Zealand	nil (did not tour)
1951 home to South Africa	two out of five
1951–52 tour to India	nil (did not tour)
1952 home to India	four out of four
1953 home to Australia	three out of five
1953–54 tour to West Indies	four out of five
1954 home to Pakistan	one out of four
1955 home to South Africa	one out of five
1956 home to Australia	five out of five
1956–57 tour to South Africa	five out of five
1957 home to West Indies	four out of five
1958 home to New Zealand	four out of five
1958–59 tour to Australia	four out of five

Explanations for some of the gaps in this international record come in a variety of ways. In the earlier stages of Jim's career the selectors sometimes decided to go into a Test with only one spinner (e.g., and much to their regret, Headingley, 1948).

Leg-spinners enjoyed a certain vogue at that time and sometimes we find one being paired with a slow left-armer (e.g. The Oval, 1948 – Eric Hollies and Jack Young; and the same pairing at Headingley and Lord's, 1949). Occasionally we find two leg-break bowlers paired together (e.g. Hollies and Roley Jenkins at Trent Bridge in 1950) and even two slow left-armers plus a leg-spinner (Lord's, 1950 – Jenkins, Johnny Wardle and Bob Berry). At a time when county sides regarded it as unthinkable to field an imbalanced side, with one spinner who turned the ball away from the bat and one who moved it in to the batsman, the England selectors so often ignored what was generally regarded as a basic principle of a properly balanced attack.

Next, let us consider the greater degree of competition for specialist places in a Test side than we have seen certainly in the past decade. The earliest contender for an England place in the Laker era of off-spinning was Brian Close, the boy-wonder of Yorkshire who arrived on the scene in the summer of 1949 when he was capped by England before he had been similarly ennobled by his own county. (We shall return to that particular claim in more detail in a moment.) Then came Roy Tattersall, of Lancashire (debut in Australia, 1951), followed by Jim McConnon, of Glamorgan (v Pakistan, 1954), Bob Appleyard (Yorkshire) in the same series, Fred Titmus (v South Africa, 1955) and Ray Illingworth, of Yorkshire (v New Zealand, 1958). Waiting in the wings were the Gloucestershire pair, John Mortimore (who played in the final Test of the 1958–59 tour to Australia) and David Allen (who had to wait until the West Indies tour of 1959–60) together with Worcestershire's Martin Horton whose batting, certainly at Test level, was probably better than his bowling. He was, nevertheless, an off-spinning rival whose batting ability was bound to commend him to some extent to the selectors. When, in the first summer after his return from the Australian tour he had yearned for, Jim found the selectors pairing together a brace of off-spinners which did not include him (Close-Mortimore, Illingworth-Mortimore v India in 1959), Jim was finally sickened by it all. It had been a continuous struggle to fight for his place over so many years; he had so many times been passed over for bowlers he regarded, understandably, as being infinitely less in ability and stature; his incredible performances of barely three years ago which had made him the best-known bowler in the world seemed now to count for little or nothing in the eyes of the selectors. He was 37 and, like many others, had lost five years of cricket to the war (although in one sense it had really developed his own cricket).

Jim knew that Tom Goddard, that great Gloucestershire off-spinner, had topped the first-class averages only 10 years earlier with 160 wickets at 19.18, when he was 48 years old. It was not age which was a governing factor in his decision. First of all it was the problem of his arthritic spinning finger, but there was also a major disillusionment with the treatment he received. He had lost his appetite for the game, his sense of enjoyment, which was so much more a part of cricket in his time than it was to become later. Very few players of his day finished a season without a whole catalogue of pleasant memories of the preceding four months. The memories might not, in every case, encompass a series of spectacular successes with bat or ball but there was usually something to recall with a smile, with a laugh, with a fond backward glance. Ask any player of 20, 30 and 40 years ago what inspired his abiding affection for cricket and the answer, almost invariably will be, 'Well, it wasn't for the money – that's for certain.' And when Jim Laker felt his sense of enjoyment had deserted him it was time to get out. It was when he began to look at the game from an entirely different angle that, happily, it returned.

Is there any logical explanation why he had played such a relatively small number of Tests? If there is, it is difficult, and Jim sought for it as much as anyone else, as much in anger as sorrow. While he felt very strongly in 1950 that he had been wrongly passed over for a place in the tour party to Australia, he was particularly angry that the man – he was really little more than a boy – who got the off-spinner's place was the 19-year-old Close. In 1949, Close had startled the cricket world by doing the double while he was still only 18 and playing for England against New Zealand at Old Trafford when, in fact, he got the selectors' vote over Laker. It was an undistinguished debut for the youngster – one wicket for 85 in the match and no runs! – and he had earned the mistrust of his captain (Freddie Brown) at a very early stage in his career. Wanting quick runs, Brown had told Close: 'Have a look at a couple, then give it a go.' This was taken absolutely literally by Close who played precisely two balls back to the slow left-armer, Tom Burtt, and was then caught at long on going for a six-hit! F. R. Brown was not terribly impressed and, in Close's view, 'had it in for him' thereafter. So this contrasts strangely with a story Jim then heard about the selectors' meeting to pick the team for the Australian tour of 1950–51.

It went like this, according to Jim himself in his book, *Over to Me*:

Various names were mentioned until someone, without much con- viction, brought up the subject of Brian Close. The subject, mentioned on an impulse, was about to be as quickly dropped, when Freddie Brown, the captain, chimed in: 'Close is the man for me; I want him,' was said to be the gist of Brown's remarks. Chirpy as ever, Brown had his way, rather to the discomfiture of the others present. Perhaps they had the sort of guilty feeling of a man who looks at some disaster and thinks, 'Did I do that?'

It might well have lingered in Jim's mind merely as a rumour and remained as nothing more than that, so that natural disappointment mingled with mild resentment but for a remarkable piece of selectorial indiscretion. Jim had opted to join that winter a tour of India undertaken by a mixed-nationality team playing under the banner of a Commonwealth XI and the captain was Leslie Ames, the former Kent and England wicketkeeper-batsman, who at that time was an England selector. At a break (Port Said) in the passage to India, Laker asked Ames about the rumour and was told (again I quote *Over to Me*): 'Your story is quite true – but you shouldn't know about it.' What happened to the doctrine of collective responsibility?

It becomes an even more incredible story when you look at Close's version of his trip to Australia, which he called 'a tour of misery'. He had rows with Brown, and with the vice-captain, Denis Compton, and by January he 'felt like a leper'. Nearly 40 years on Close recalls the experience with bitterness: 'I went out to Australia a naive and unworldly boy. Many times I retired dejectedly to my room at the end of the day, in sheer misery at the wall of hostility built by men I had hero-worshipped for years.' So if it is indeed correct that Freddie Brown had opted for Close's selection over Jim Laker (and the possible alternative, Roy Tattersall who was, in fact, flown out later to join the party) it suggests some very odd thinking in the selection room and even odder tour-captaincy.

On figures the selection could not be justified because Laker in the summer of 1950 had taken 166 wickets at 15.32 while Close had taken 20 for 19.30 but, as happens with great frequency, figures can be misleading. Close was doing national service in the Army by this time and his playing opportunities, therefore, were limited. Also, the selectors may well have reflected, he was not only an all-rounder with left-handed batting of tremendous promise, but he was a two-in-one bowler who could deliver fast-medium seamers as well as off-breaks. So it is possible for the selectors to make out a case for their choice even if it is equally possible to point out jagged flaws in it. England had suffered a tremendous mauling in Australia in 1946–47 and another in England in 1948. It can be cogently argued that the situation called for experience and expertise rather than youthful enthusiasm and promise.

In 1954–55, the selectors' choice for Australia was Jim McConnon and on figures this time there was not much in it. Laker, sixth in the first-class averages that summer, had 135 wickets at 15.17, and McConnon, one place behind him, took 109 at 15.41. But this was Len Hutton's tour and he had firm ideas on the sort of side he needed to hold on to the Ashes his team had regained in 1953. He was going for an all-out pace attack and while there was no suggestion of another bodyline tour England's first professional captain certainly did not discount the idea of achieving a physical domination on the faster, bouncier Australian wickets. So the men upon whom Hutton was primarily going to rely were Frank Tyson, then the fastest bowler in the world, Alec Bedser, Brian Statham and Trevor Bailey. More to the point, also in the party was Bob Appleyard who had taken 154 wickets at 14.42 that summer and could not only reinforce the pace attack with his swing and seam bowling but could switch to off-spinners if required. Once again, J. C. Laker was being usurped by a fellow-Yorkshireman who was a dual-purpose bowler. There must have seemed to him a certain irony in this.

The additional selection of McConnon, therefore, seems rather strange, especially with Johnny Wardle in the party. He was certainly going to be the front-line spinner if the occasion arose to use a specialist slow bowler. Even after a serious misjudgement of the pitch had led Hutton to put Australia in and concede the First Test by the massive margin of an innings and 154 runs, his side had won the rubber by the end of the Fourth. With the series in the bag and incessant heavy rain pounding New South Wales, McConnon still did not get into the Final Test side and – given Hutton's clearly defined policy on that tour – it has to be seen as improbable that Laker would have found a place if he had been in the party. Yet he felt he should have gone and on known form at the time of selection and his high reputation, he undoubtedly had a point. It is interesting to note that another Yorkshireman bitterly disappointed to miss that tour was F. S. Trueman.

And so to 1958–59 when Jim finally found a place in a touring party to Australia, a trip he had coveted – as all Test cricketers did – since he first represented England. His natural cricketing ambition to play there had been strengthened by a visit at the end of his 1951–52 coaching spell in New Zealand when he and Lilly flew to Australia in one of those wonderful old Sunderland flying-boats, and then did the grand tour of

Sydney, Melbourne, Adelaide, Perth, before sailing back to England — in the company of Ray Lindwall and his wife.

His claims to a place on tour were this time unassailable. On psychological grounds alone he had to go to Australia while the wounds he had inflicted two summers earlier were still unhealed. In the English season he had taken 116 wickets at 14.23 (it had been a tremendous season for his partner, Tony Lock, too, with 34 Test wickets against New Zealand and 170 first-class victims in all), 17 of them in Tests where he appeared in four out of five. And yet once again Jim almost did not go to Australia, though this time the reasons were nothing to do with the selectors.

On 8 July he took part in a remarkable Test at Headingley which England won inside the last three days, no play having been possible on the first two. In the first innings Laker's figures were 22-11-17-5 and in the second he returned 36-23-27-3. It was a game I remember rather well because of Bill Playle's innings of 18 in New Zealand's second knock — it took just under three-and-three-quarter hours and I have always been very glad not to have been commentating on it! At the end of the Test the Surrey contingent (Laker, Lock and May) set out in convoy to drive to Swansea for the next county championship match and *en route* May's car broke down. It is not difficult to imagine with what delight the two bowlers, who between them had got through nearly 112 overs (and taken 19 wickets), now faced the prospect of pushing their captain's car in search of help. There were no motorways to speed their progress once May's car had been restored to working order, and the trio arrived in Wales at 3 a.m. As surely as night follows day, May lost the toss and so a largely sleepless night was followed by a long day in the field. Jim bowled 63 overs against Glamorgan, another 54 in the following match against Kent and not unnaturally the spinning finger was now beginning to show distinct signs of wear and tear.

Now in the modern era where the emphasis in English, Australian and West Indian cricket is distinctly on pace bowling it is not easy for the younger generation of followers of the game to appreciate the extent to which sore spinning fingers affected the slower bowlers of 25 and 30 years ago. Wickets were uniformly truer in those days; new balls, without the present polyurethane coating, did not retain their shine long into the day. Once the shine had gone, it was the spinners' job to plug the gap until the next one was due. If the wicket was drying or dusting, fair enough — the spinners cashed in. But if the pitch remained good — well, there was a lot of hard labour to be undertaken. In the course of eight consecutive days' play, Laker had bowled 175 overs.

Consider now, if you will, that in the 1986 and 1987 seasons the only off-spinner to feature in the leading first-class averages was Jack Simmons, of Lancashire. And he bowled just 230.5 overs in the whole of the 1986 season. And bear in mind, too, that Laker spun the ball immensely more vigorously than Simmons. In fact Jim gave it a tremendous flick of the fingers so that the contact of two digits in particular with the constantly coarsening seam of the ageing ball was bound to have its effect. There was no known treatment for this kind of injury. Spinners used constantly to anoint tender fingers with friar's balsam in an attempt to toughen up the skin but I cannot recall a single case where this was anything other than a matter of fighting a losing battle.

So when Jim met his captain at The Oval immediately after the Kent match (which had been lost) at Blackheath in 1958 and Peter May said, 'I don't think you were trying to bowl them out,' Jim's reaction was predictably one of outrage. It was, as he recalled the remark, 'damn near to slander'. To someone as professional in his approach to his bowling as Jim Laker one can only marvel that he qualified his view to 'damn near'. It is possible – just possible – that in the middle of that concentrated succession of bowling days Jim might have seemed to his captain to be less than 100 per cent enthusiastic about the job in hand. We have all seen occasions when great bowlers have reached a point at which immediate success seems unlikely. Great batting can create that sort of situation; so can pitches with neither bounce nor turn; just occasionally a hopeless position in a game can produce it, too. But it takes a very brave, or foolhardy, critic to tell a great bowler he is not actually trying. Jim Laker was one of the least volatile players I have ever seen. He was not a demonstrative man by nature and not even Old Trafford, 1956, induced anything beyond a flicker of a grin. My broadcasting colleague, Brian Johnston, recalls that when he walked across from the commentary box at the end of the match to invite Jim to be interviewed he seemed 'the least excited person in the dressing-room'. England colleague Alan Oakman confirmed the view. So it is not surprising if he did not radiate wild enthusiasm at Blackheath when bowling his 175th over in eight days. But ... not trying? That was something else altogether and J. C. Laker was having none of it.

I am a Yorkshireman, [he wrote of that encounter with May], I learned my cricket in the ruthless school of the League and it comes naturally to me to try. Even in the friendliest of Benefit matches I don't feel comfortable if I can't be working all the time to get the most wickets for the fewest runs. I don't claim this as a virtue. It's just a habit, deeply ingrained - and a habit which I believe, in passing, to have contributed to whatever successes I have enjoyed.

An observation of Mickey Stewart is relevant at this point because Stewart, as a short-leg fieldsman, was a particularly involved partner of his on the field as well as a good friend off it:

I have heard the criticism that Jim didn't care, or gave the impression of not trying his utmost at times. If the conditions were not right, if the ball was not turning on a particular day, it was possible to get that impression. Now I believe – and I said this to him – that he was by nature quite an emotional and sensitive individual so he had deliberately schooled himself to walk around in a way, at a particular pace so that it would seem to those who didn't know him well that he was indifferent to what was happening. Don't you believe it. He cared; he always cared.

May's remark suggests that the captain did not understand entirely the Laker attitude and that in itself is a trifle strange since they were something more than Surrey and England colleagues. Laker, at any rate, regarded them at that time as having a relationship of personal friendship. So the debate which ensued was 'fairly heated', and it was unresolved when they parted. It rankled with Jim and, not to put too fine a point on it, he brooded about the exchange not only in its own context but in the much wider one of probably going to Australia the following winter with May as his captain. Jim was on the list of those players who had been approached about their availability and had said 'Yes'. There seemed no reason to expect anyone other than May to lead the side in Australia. The more Jim thought about May's remark, the angrier he became and with the captain refusing a request for the 'slander' to be withdrawn his anger exacerbated the situation within his own mind. He informed the Surrey secretary, Commander Bob Babb, that he was now not available to tour and – astonishing though it seems now – the Commander did not question the decision or dwell on the reasons for it, but telephoned Lord's immediately to pass on the information. At Headquarters there was no disposition to query the message, either, and a brief statement was issued to the press. *Fait accompli*. J. C. Laker would not be going to Australia.

It couldn't happen today, of course. The Test and County Cricket

Board are very much more sensitive to public opinion and to press reaction than MCC were in 1958. Looking back on these events from the late eighties it seems odd that it should happen so peremptorily, especially when 200 miles to the north all hell broke loose about that time when Yorkshire decided to dispense with the services of Johnny Wardle just after *he* had been picked for the Australian tour. The essential difference in the two cases was, of course, that Johnny's grievances against his captain were aired in the *Daily Mail* while Jim's were kept within the Surrey family. But it is nevertheless startling to learn that his 'non-availability' was accepted without comment from either the Surrey secretary or the MCC hierarchy. Laker himself had, perhaps, been a little precipitate in making his decision and a sort of chain reaction followed. But why had no one asked any questions? *That* certainly couldn't happen today!

With Jim hurt and angry at what he regarded as an unjustified slight by his captain and Peter May apparently unwilling to withdraw his allegation, the situation was to all intents and purposes an impasse. It is a measure of the depth of Jim's resentment that after his great disappointment at being passed over by the selectors in 1950–51 and again in 1954–55 and his very keen desire to play in an Australian tour, he was nevertheless still willing to refuse the 1958–59 tour because of this unresolved dispute. Apart from his formal, written intimation that he would be available, he had given a verbal, informal assurance to Gubby Allen, then chairman of the selectors, that he was ready to tour, so this was something of an additional embarrassment.

It was finally resolved in something of an accidental way. While Jim was discussing the matter with his agent, Denis Compton happened to be on the same premises and became involved in the debate. Jim confessed to having regrets that the problem had arisen and the state it had reached but insisted that he did not want to tour under a captain who thought he was a shirker. It is pretty obvious that he had expected questions to be asked when the cancellation of his acceptance reached Lord's and he was far from happy that it had been announced in the press, apparently without anyone in MCC asking why. The discussion in agent Bagenel Harvey's office ended with Denis Compton telephoning S. C. ('Billy') Griffiths, assistant secretary to the MCC, and suggesting a clear-the-air meeting involving May, Allen and Ronnie Aird, the MCC secretary. This duly took place, but after Laker had aired his grievance, May still refused to withdraw his 'not-trying' allegation. While Jim got the impression that Gubby Allen at least had some sympathy with him it was obviously a tricky matter actually to order the England captain to withdraw. The well-known British compromise outcome to the meeting was a suggestion that May and Laker should talk it over again. They did this the following day at The Oval but still May declined to back down. By this time at least one journalist had guessed (or been informed) what was behind the Laker withdrawal and speculation was beginning to develop in other newspapers. Jim was becoming less keen by the minute on the Australian trip and more fed up with the situation. Another day went by and another meeting took place at The Oval. This time May said he had been thinking deeply about the whole affair and suggested Jim should 'forget he had ever said anything' about the match at Blackheath. Laker was glad to accept the olive branch and so went on tour to Australia – at last. Next came MCC's withdrawal of the invitation to Wardle to tour (arising out of his *Daily Mail* articles) and so the partnership of Laker and Lock was to be re-established.

It is now 30 years since these events took place and one cannot help marvelling at the way the game has changed in such a relatively short space of time. Not the least of these changes, by any means, has been the relationship between players and administrators. 'Player power' was a substantial force by 1988 and discussions between players, selectors, the TCCB itself are conducted on a pretty democratic basis; in 1958, with MCC running the show, the situation was, by comparison, almost feudal. If selecting Laker as a player, while without doubt he still resented a slight from the man who was to be his tour captain, was potentially dangerous; putting him as well under the management of Freddie Brown was potentially explosive. But clearly the MCC in 1958 did not even contemplate rebelliousness in their contracted players and perhaps they were justified since threats of a players' 'strike' (Pakistan, 1978) and a statement of support of their captain (Pakistan again, 1987) when disciplinary action against Mike Gatting was very much a possibility, would have been unthinkable 30 years earlier.

It is never particularly satisfactory to print only one side of an argument (or in this case, two) so I asked both Freddie Brown and Peter May in writing for their views on the criticisms which Jim later expressed about both of them concerning events in the 1950s. Mr Brown replied, 'Not having read one word of J.C.L.'s book I am not prepared to comment but thank you for giving me the chance.' Mr May telephoned to say, with great courtesy, that he felt nothing could be gained by re-opening old controversies.

While one naturally accepts Freddie Brown's word that he did not read *Over to Me*, it is just a bit difficult to believe that he can have been completely unaware of its contents, which were headlined in most of the country's leading newspapers at the time. Moreover before publication of the book itself, parts of it – the most critical parts, naturally – were serialised in the *Empire News*, one of a clutch of Kemsley newspapers which used to be published in Manchester. Laker's criticisms may appear mild by modern standards but in 1960 they were nothing short of sensational – a *professional* cricketer having the effrontery to voice complaints about *two* amateur captains! Sensational is probably an inadequate word if the occasion is seen in context. To add fuel to the fire, Jim vigorously defended his book against all comers: Was it an 'attack' to say the MCC made a mistake in sending *two* managers to Australia? Was it wrong to say press relations on the tour (to Australia) were bad? Was it wrong for him to claim that Surrey did not treat their professionals as they ought to do? Why did the county never attempt to find winter employment for young players when there were so many influential businessmen amongst the Surrey membership who were not even approached to help? If all this was not made public by someone, Jim insisted, the cricketing public would never know of the conditions under which members of the staff had to earn their living.

Undoubtedly the book drew attention to many points which were unknown to the lay membership of county clubs. There was at that time a tendency for us simply to envy the professionals for their ability, and the opportunity to play their cricket at such an exalted level, without pausing to think that it might not all be a bed of roses. *Over to Me* turned over a number of flat stones and the MCC in particular did not like the creepie-crawlies which were revealed. The Surrey club – which was later to change dramatically, let it be said, with much ex-player involvement at Committee level – were, if anything, more furious than the moguls at Lord's. Laker's honorary membership of MCC was withdrawn – the most condign punishment that august body could conjure up – and he became *persona non grata* at The Oval as well. Not until 1967 when tempers had cooled, memories had dimmed, and attitudes had become more liberal were the honours restored. It is not difficult to see that at times Jim nurtured a love-hate relationship with some aspects of cricket, though never with the game itself.

In some ways he was perhaps ahead of his time, and not the least of these were the workings of his lively and inquiring mind, allied to that touch of rebelliousness. This is not to say that the majority of his contemporaries were unintelligent by any means but Jim applied the same reasoning processes which he brought to his bowling when it came to the wider aspects of his cricketing life. He questioned things which authority felt were not within the province of a professional, a mercenary. He asked questions which were sometimes unanswerable and authority was never going to enjoy that. It was this side of the man which was highlighted brilliantly in a monograph by John Arlott, with whom he formed an understandable mutual admiration society:

If Jim Laker is to be credited with one outstanding attribute, it must be that of intelligence; and not merely intelligence but *applied* intelligence. There have been thoughtful off-spin bowlers in recent years whose ideas often led them to cling stubbornly to uneconomic methods of attack. From Jim Laker's intelligence, however, stemmed other assets: it produced, importantly, the observation, judgement and flexibility which enabled him so rapidly to assess changing circumstances and change his method to suit them. Tom Goddard was, to an entire generation, the personification of the off-spinner: Laker himself had an admiration for him. But Goddard was essentially an attacking bowler. On responsive pitches he was a killer; but he often persisted in attacking on an unhelpful pitch or against a batsman who had his measure when, in his and his side's best interests, it would have been better to apply the curbs of restrictive length, line and field-setting. This was a mistake Jim Laker hardly ever made. Given the right conditions – or, as in his triumph at Old Trafford, even *half-right* conditions – he could be a destroyer. On the other hand, when the pitch favoured batsmen, he could bowl so tightly as to confine the best of them and fret them into self-destroying error. He did so, with sustained effect – and perhaps most surprisingly – in the West Indies in 1947–48 at the very outset of his career when he was quite raw; and, as is more often remembered, in 1958–59 when the Australian batsmen, remembering their indignities of 1956, were grimly bent on revenge on their own pitches.

Few, especially among his opponents, would dispute that Jim Laker was the finest of his own, or probably any, period. It was not a simple coincidence that the years of his maturity were also a period of success for both his county and his country. Yet it would do him less justice to overlook the fact that he produced some of his most sustained and skilful bowling in losing sides. Both his figures and style argued that he was unusually mature at the very outset of his first-class career and still unquestionably a great bowler at its end.

Memory will recall him very English-looking, six feet tall, firmly built, fair-haired, fresh-faced, quiet in demeanour, coming up to the bowler's end, his shoulders hunched, cap at a jaunty angle. He moved to his bowling mark at a constabular stroll and with the laconic air of one with his tongue in his cheek pattered along a run of artfully varied short strides. Then, wrist and arm cocked, he swung through a model, high delivery-arc into the positive follow-through which generated so much spin and life.

That is very much the way many of us saw Laker but few have had the ability to express it so felicitously. The genius of Arlott, journalist or commentator, lay in the touch of romance, and sometimes mysticism, with which he could invest an essentially practical operation. He did it without excessive adventures into hyperbole but by his search for the *mot just* which, for him, was rarely a laboured pursuit. It came so naturally that many of us, sitting alongside John in the commentary box, have marvelled at the ease of it all.

And so the phrase which leaps out from that Arlott passage – to me, at any rate – is '... when the pitch favoured batsmen he could bowl so tightly as to confine the best of them and fret them into self-destroying error'. It recalled a long conversation I once had with Jim about Hedley Verity, who, it seemed to both of us in our childhood days watching at Headingley or Park Avenue, had refined the art and science of slow left-arm bowling to as near perfection as is humanly possible. J. M. Kilburn, distinguished cricket correspondent of the *Yorkshire Post* before and after the Second World War, knew Verity's bowling intimately and once wrote:

In Verity's cricketing philosophy the easy triumph was not the most satisfying. To dismiss a modest batting side on a turning pitch was to him no more than the routine of a bank cashier completing a simple balance. It was a professional obligation. Failure, or unnecessary delay, would have been professional weakness. Verity's idea of cricketing heaven was to bowl against Australia – with Bradman, of course – not when conditions left batsmen helpless but when one factor offered the bowler opportunity. A small, rough patch on the wicket, an encouraging breeze, a time element, something first of all to be discerned, then exploited, with success or failure delicately balanced, gave Verity his greatest cricket inspiration and joy. He wanted a challenge for his bowling mind as well as for his fingers. There were times in county cricket when he appeared to be deliberately making the game harder for himself by insisting on achievement in a pre-determined manner; when he seemed to spend three overs preparing an lbw snare against a batsman who, unharrassed, would probably have mishit into the covers anyway.

I had read that some time in the mid-seventies and enjoyed it so much – as a kind of *bel canto* of cricket literature – that I had committed it, or most of it, to memory rather like the wodges of Shakespeare some of us have retained in the mind since schooldays, and in the context of my conversation now with Jim, I trotted it out. He pondered in silence for a moment, then grinned, 'I don't think I could have put it much better myself.' But we both knew, and appreciated, superb writing about a superb bowler.

When I put it to Jim it was a reasonable reflection of his own bowling attitude, however, he would have none of it. 'You are not asking me to compare myself with Verity, are you?' he demanded with something of a snarl. This was not false modesty, and it was not natural modesty so much as an acute embarrassment at being asked to discuss any mani-festation of his own outstanding ability. He simply couldn't do it and, on reflection, one had to see that as understandable. Jim sought refuge in unfavourable comparison: 'It didn't look much like that at Headingley in 1948, did it?'

That Fourth Test in 1948 against, arguably, the greatest of all Aus-tralian touring sides was always Jim's prime example when he indulged in self-criticism. He felt strongly that he had not bowled well enough against a side which was required to score more than 400 in the fourth innings on a pitch which was taking spin *to a limited degree* because it was dusty after four days on which 1,319 runs had already been scored. So it wasn't a bad pitch, by any means. Jim felt he ought to have done more in restricting Australia's brilliant second innings in which Morris scored 182 and Bradman 173 not out as they raced to 404 for three wickets and his bowling figures were 32-11-93-0. There are three points on which to base a view that Jim was too hard on himself, as I see it: (1) It was only his third Test in England and his bowling had not reached a stage of refinement which was to mark it in the following decade; (2) England had taken a calculated risk by going in without a second spinner and Compton's occasional Chinamen and Hutton's even more occasional leg-spinners were the only support available; (3) the batting of Bradman and Morris, who put together 301 in 217 minutes, was quite, quite magnificent and provided one of the most enthralling day's cricket I have ever seen. Even Verity knew days when it was absolutely impossible for him to curb the flow (Headingley, 1934, for example), but Verity would certainly have approved of Laker's soul-searching after the 1948 defeat – more thought to be applied, more lessons to be learned. But nearly 40 years later, Jim still sought the answer to his lack of success in Leeds on 27 July, 1948. And this in spite of his knowledge that Bradman had been missed behind the stumps early on. Just over a year later, in a letter to Jim, the Don confessed, 'If Godfrey Evans had been' a little more alert I would have been a spectator for most of the Test and you would have been the cause of it.'

There was no comparison, says Trevor Bailey, between the callow off-spinner who played against the Australians in 1948 and the polished artist he became later. Perhaps Laker was unlucky to be chosen at this stage, before he was fully ready for international cricket, since it may have been the cause of the selectors subsequently taking so long to appreciate his talents. But looking at those talents and comparing them with those of some of the men who followed him one is prompted to ask once again: did the selectors *ever* 'fully appreciate' his worth? To descend to one of the oldest clichés in the language, that about comparisons being odious, we saw John Emburey in 1987 being picked for five Tests against Pakistan (even though he was left out from the original 12 in one match) and not taking a single wicket, yet being automatically selected for three different parties to tour during the following winter and made vice-captain as well. The following summer, after Mike Gatting had been relieved of the captaincy after the First Test (for reasons unconnected with his cricket), Emburey was the man the selectors turned to for a skipper in the next two Tests against the most powerful opposition in the world. He was still being played as the country's number one spin bowler. Jim Laker did not live to see these events but he knew perfectly well that as far back as 1981 Emburey was regularly referred to, in English circles at any rate, as 'the best off-spinner in the world' when he returned from a winter tour in the West Indies with figures of 185-62-419-7 (avge 59.85) after playing in all four Tests. Never once did I hear J. C. Laker criticise the regular selection of Emburey; never did I hear him knock Emburey's bowling. On the contrary, he frequently expressed support for the Middlesex off-spinner and if he could not find something good to say he usually refrained from comment. He would not have approved of my making the comparison, either, but a statistical coincidence makes it irresistible when one considers that at the end of the 1987 season John Emburey had played in 46 Tests –

exactly the same number as Jim Laker. Their respective figures were then:

Laker: 12,027 deliveries, 4,101 runs, 193 wickets, 21.24 average. Five wickets in an innings nine times; 10 wickets in a match three times

Emburey: 10,868 deliveries, 3,855 runs, 115 wickets, 33.52 average. Five wickets in an innings six times; ten wickets in a match, never

During the major part of his career, Emburey's rivals for the off-spinner's place in England sides have been Eddie Hemmings, of Nottinghamshire, and Geoff Miller, when he was with Derbyshire.

Laker's contemporaries were more numerous and, in the days of uncovered wickets, generally more successful than Emburey's and Jim was the first to say that the covering of pitches would have created greater difficulties for him as a bowler. On the other hand Test cricket was played in his day on infinitely better pitches than we have seen in say, the past 10 years. Test wickets were expected to be good batting wickets with a bit of pace in them and the spinner was normally expected to come into his own later in the game when the pitch was worn and, perhaps, a little dusty. Bowling, therefore, was regarded as harder work and requiring a higher degree of skill than has generally been the case in the 1980s. If any further evidence of this is required then a glance at first-class (and even more particularly Test) averages in the past decade will provide it. Spinners have virtually disappeared from the game at top level and when, at Old Trafford in 1988, a Test pitch was expected to give help to slow bowlers an almost frenzied search took place to find a suitable slow left-arm partner for Emburey. (The result of the game, a huge win for the West Indies, was indicative in almost equal proportions to (1) the supremacy of West Indian *fast* bowling; (2) the decline of English batsmanship; (3) the ineffectiveness of spin bowling in an age when it had largely gone out of fashion. Denis Compton was moved to comment that Laker and Lock would have bowled out West Indies for a very low score indeed on that pitch. Instead, they were able to declare at a mere 384 for seven and win by an innings and 156 runs.

That is a view which would undoubtedly find favour with G.A.R. Lock, whose view of modern spinners is typically trenchant: 'I call them "slow bowlers" because I cannot bring myself to call them *spin* bowlers. No one in the past 20 to 25 years has been fit to lace Jim Laker's boots. I'd like to use stronger words but let's just say they are pretty hopeless.'

Trevor Bailey was England's first great post-war all round cricketer and played 61 times for England. Since retiring he has become one of the outstanding professional observers of the game and his views are based on more than 30 years of close personal involvement in it. He also played alongside Laker and was, in fact, in his leg-trap at the Test Trial fiasco at Bradford in 1950. His view of the man must, therefore, be absolutely authoritative:

First, he had exceptional control. Accuracy of line and length is the fundamental of all categories of bowling but to none is it more important than the off-spinner. On occasions a fast full toss will take a wicket while many a batsman has holed out off a leg-breaking long hop but the off-spinner cannot afford inaccuracies of this nature because he has to rely so much on his short-leg fieldsmen who must be prepared to stand perilously close to the batsman. A bad ball immediately puts them in considerable danger. Even if they avoid being hit, a series of indifferent deliveries will very quickly destroy their confidence. Then they will edge away instead of forward and so greatly reduce their effectiveness. Short-leg has never been my favour-ite position but I was always happy to stand there for Jim Laker as his control reduced my chances of being struck to a minimum. I found I could afford to station myself considerably closer to the wicket than with any other bowler of his type. This made all the difference when trying to make a catch off a purely defensive stroke. [We must remember, moreover, that no protective helmets were used in those days.]

Second, Laker's body action was almost classical. He looked over the left arm, came down on a braced left leg, swivelled and even dug a pit with his left foot. Third, he spun his off break sufficiently to make it turn on perfect pitches. Fourth, he was equally at home over or round the wicket. When he was abroad he operated chiefly from over but on a pitch responsive to turn he went round. Fifth, he had the ability to make the ball leave the bat off the pitch without any perceptible change of action. I was not alone in being unable to pick the one that 'went with his arm'. His subtle variations of flight and spin were a continued source of delight to the connoisseur. He learned to recognise and exploit the foibles of individual batsmen and was able to adapt his techniques to different circumstances. Although his rewards were inevitably greater on a 'sticky' or a 'crumbler', Jim was still liable to worry the finest players in the world on that hard, fast batting paradise at Sabina Park in Kingston, Jamaica. 'Big Jim' Laker was the finest off-spinner I have played with or against.

And so say just about all his contemporaries or, to put it another way, if there were any who differed from Bailey's view they have remained rather quiet about it.

TOURING DAYS

Although Jim was very much a family man – a devoted father and, later, grandfather – almost paradoxically he was an enthusiastic tourist and traveller. It is unlikely that his service in Egypt had given him a taste for foreign travel because the average serviceman's memories of that country in wartime were not particularly fond ones but certainly his call at Durban on the way out to the Middle East made a distinctly favourable impression. Was there a member of any branch of the Forces who didn't think the same way? From bomb-battered, blacked-out and austerity-streamlined Britain, those who survived the U-boat attacks sailed into a country where the hospitality was overwhelming, where the lights shone brightly at night and the shops were filled with all the luxury goods which were not seen at home. A 19-year-old, abroad for the first time, could scarcely fail to want to return to such a land. No one mentioned apartheid in those days; not too many people in or from Britain were aware of it and most of those who were did not pay much attention. Jim did indeed return, as a coach and as an England tourist and his views on life there changed as he saw a different country from the one he had known on his sorties from the troopship. We shall come to that in due course.

He was an adaptable man, clearly, because I rarely heard a moan from Jim about conditions on his tour of India in the winter of 1950–51 although they were utterly primitive when compared with those experienced by the 1988 tourists to neighbouring Pakistan – who were given a tour bonus of £1,000 a man to compensate for the 'privations' they felt they had suffered. In 1950–51 there were hotels of a reasonable standard in the merest handful of cities; travel was by noisy, crowded, slow-moving trains and eating was usually a gastronomical form of Russian roulette. And yet Laker enjoyed his tour with the Commonwealth team gathered together by George Duckworth, the pre-war Lancashire and England wicketkeeper. Short and dumpy, 'Duckie' was one of the great characters of the game as a player and afterwards endeared himself to MCC touring sides as scorer, baggagemaster, general factotum and fixer. When he was not touring he worked as a BBC commentator on Rugby League with great success. For the tour to India he assembled what Jim often described as 'just about the best cricket team I ever played with'.

Les Ames was nominally captain but did not play in many games and the side was usually led by Frank Worrell. Apart from his brilliant batsmanship, Worrell (who was knighted in 1964 for his services to cricket) was a useful opening bowler, left-arm fast-medium, and an excellent close-to-the-wicket fieldsman. He was also a man of great personal charm and quite the best tactician and on-the-field director of operations the West Indies have ever had, in my view. His batting strength in India was headed by Harold Gimblett (Somerset), Laurie Fishlock (Surrey) and George Emmett (Gloucestershire) followed by Ken Grieves, the Australian who later skippered Lancashire, and his team-mate Jack Ikin. The quick bowling was in the hands of Les Jackson (Derbyshire), Fred Ridgeway (Kent), Derek Shackleton (Hampshire) and Worrell himself − but what about the spin attack? Laker, Bruce Dooland (the brilliant Australian leg-spinner who played for Nottinghamshire), Sonny Ramadhin, the little wizard from Trinidad who had tortured England's batsmen the previous summer, and George Tribe, another Australian who played for Northamptonshire and was one of the most accomplished unorthodox slow left-armers the game has ever seen. It certainly was a formidable side and it went through 27 tour matches unbeaten.

Before and since that tour, players of high calibre have fairly consistently turned down invitations to visit the sub-continent, in some cases risking their Test futures to do so. Conditions in India and Pakistan have become progressively better as more money has been invested in the building of western-style hotels but in 1950–51 they must have been chronically bad. Yet I cannot recall J. C. Laker talking about that tour in critical tones. He would tell stories about those days, yes, but inevitably for the entertainment and amusement of others − not as a means of conjuring up the horrors of touring there. Obviously, Duckworth's party were a happy band of touring pilgrims who blended well together and rejoiced in each other's company. That is the way happy tour memories are born. And it has to be remembered that Laker joined that party at a time of bitter disappointment when he was passed over for the MCC trip to Australia. If he went in a disgruntled state of mind it was not obvious to anyone who toured with him and talked about the trip in later days.

His first tour had, of course, been to the West Indies after barely a season in first-class cricket and it, too, had stimulated his interest in travelling.

Life has changed at a bewildering rate since the Second World War and I find a personal fascination in dwelling upon some aspects of it. For a tour to West Indies these days one flies from Gatwick in a TriStar aircraft or Jumbo 747 jet and arrives in Barbados in less than half a day, yet on Jim Laker's first tour the party sailed from Liverpool in a 4,000-ton banana boat and was bounced around in Atlantic gales for nearly a fortnight before disembarking. Their stipend for the tour was £300 out of which Winston Place, the Lancashire opening batsman, freely offered £50 to anyone who would shoot him after the first two days to end his suffering from *mal de mer*. A modern tourist would think himself poorly paid indeed if he did not make more than £10,000 for a trip of similar duration. Jim's arrival in Barbados gave rise to one of his favourite stories — one which he told over and over again with the Brian Johnston touring road-show and it always went down well.

Jim was having a social drink with a middle-aged chap when he learned that he was talking to one of the umpires who would stand in the Tests. Making sure that the glasses of rum punch kept arriving with great regularity (just about the easiest thing anyone can do in the West Indies!), Jim cultivated a relationship which quickly advanced in cordiality. Finally he moved on to talk to Clyde Walcott, the largest and most powerfully built of the Three Ws of Barbadian and West Indian Test cricket and couldn't resist a typical Lakerian jest: 'You know who that was? One of the Test umpires, and we got on very well indeed. If I were you I'd keep my legs out of the way when I'm bowling.' Walcott's face broke into a huge grin as he replied, 'If I were you I'd go back and get him another drink — he's my uncle!' And Jim's wry punchline to the story was: 'I can't remember a single lbw appeal going in my favour.'

The development of the tourist trade in the West Indies has made it one of the most popular areas for England cricket supporters in recent years. Barbados and Antigua in particular are ideal spots to combine a holiday in winter sunshine with cricket-watching — in direct contrast to actual cricket-playing as the islands have become the most potent force in the world through their seemingly inexhaustible supply of frighteningly quick bowlers. In 1947–48 few people could afford a holiday of that kind and in any case the England sides rarely included more than a sprinkling of really top-class players. So it was that Jim's first tour skipper was Gubby Allen — later to become Sir George Allen, *eminence gris* of MCC — doubling up as one of the fast bowlers at the age of 45! Small wonder, then, that he missed the first Test because of a pulled calf muscle sustained during his skipping exercises on the boat! It was, however, a notable Test debut for J. C. Laker who returned seven wickets for 103 despite being hit for 6, 6, 4, 4, by E. A. V. Williams off the first four balls he received. Jim had an awful lot of bowling to do on the tour and was quick to acknowledge that he 'learned a lot from some wonderful bowling spells by Dick Howorth,' the Worcestershire slow left-armer. His memories of the tour, at least as recounted to me, were of good cricket, good companionship, good fun. He went back to the West Indies, particularly to Barbados, many times when his playing days were over; he had many friends there, loved the relaxed lifestyle and the passionate devotion to cricket. In particular he cherished his memories of bowling at the three Ws, Worrell, Weekes and Walcott, of whom he rated Everton Weekes slightly ahead of the other two. One of the hallmarks of the great bowler is his enjoyment of bowling at great batsmen. Lesser practitioners shrink from the possibility of 'getting some tap', but in Laker one can see something of the Hedley Verity whom he admired so much. And so Jim, while still learning his trade at the highest level, had plenty of opportunity to enjoy himself on that first tour against the emerging brilliance of the Barbadian trio plus men like Jeff Stollmeyer, Gerry Gomez and the West Indian folk hero, George Headley. In the First Test at the Kensington Oval, Bridgetown, Barbados, his figures were 37–9–103–7 and 30–12–95–2. In the Second (Queen's Park, Port-of-Spain, Trinidad) 36–10–108–2. In the Third (Bourda, Georgetown, British Guiana – now Guyana) 36–11–94–2 and 9–1–34–2. In the Fourth and last (Sabina Park, Kingston, Jamaica) 36.4–5–103–3 and 2–0–11–0. Yes, there was ample scope to do a lot of learning on that tour.

After a 1951 season in which Jim took 149 first-class wickets and topped the England averages against South Africa, Roy Tattersall, of Lancashire, was the off-spinner who went on the winter tour to India and so Mr and Mrs Laker took up residence in New Zealand during the worst months of the English year and would have been there again the following winter when England had no tour but for the impending arrival of daughter Fiona.

Being passed over for another Australian tour (1954–55) was, as we have seen, another severe blow to Jim but at least he had, in the meantime, enjoyed the sunshine (and the hard work) of West Indies again in the previous winter. This time it was under the captaincy of Len Hutton so it was obviously going to be a much more businesslike affair than in 1947–48. Hutton would not have set out with a tour side half made up of inexperienced players and indeed he took a party which was as strong as England could muster. If there was a weakness at all it was in the absence of a seasoned opening batsman to partner Hutton and after improvising with Willie Watson in the first three Tests, Trevor

Bailey was called up in the last two. (In Jamaica the amazing Bailey took seven wickets for 34 in rolling over an immensely strong batting side for 139 – Gary Sobers at number nine! – then went out to open the innings.) But the match which every man on that tour remembers best of all was the Fourth Test in Port-of-Spain. May and Compton got hundreds and Graveney 92 so their memories are pleasant ones; for others in the party the pleasure was muted. In fact one might say the statistics of the game are seared on the soul. Notable amongst this group were J. C. Laker and F. S. Trueman. Fred has said, 'When I die they might as well cover my grave with a bit of jute matting because I'll swear that's what cut down my life by a year or two in Trinidad.' After nine overs, Brian Statham pulled a muscle and once again it was the resolute and uncomplaining Bailey who had to shoulder responsibility for partnering Fred's quick bowling. Umpiring shortcomings resulted in Weekes escaping four dismissals as West Indies declared at 681 for eight.

It was the first matting wicket that F. S. T. had ever seen – which was not the case with Jim Laker, of course. But this was a far cry from the matting on which he had first discovered his gift for bowling off-breaks and the opposition was a cut higher than the service personnel of Egypt, 10 years earlier. After 50 overs he had taken two wickets for 154 – and that was the best analysis of the five front-line bowlers on parade. Typically, Jim never wasted time remembering his tribulations with the ball. One of his favourite stories centred on his batting partnership with Trueman:

> After a couple of days in the field [England replied with 537] in exceptionally hot weather the West Indies were looking jaded when I was joined in the middle by Fred as the second, or possibly the third new ball was due. The one exception was Frank King, the Barbados fast bowler, who was still as lively as ever and letting loose his fair share of bouncers.
>
> Frank Worrell had taken the new ball with him and by this time Frank was hardly more than medium pace. Fred then called a mid-wicket conference and announced, 'I've assessed the situation, Jim lad, and I think if you takes King, I can look after Worrell.'

Speechless at this quite marvellous effrontery, Laker could only nod his agreement and was still dazed enough to attempt a shot which was not normally in his repertoire – the hook – when King gave him another bouncer.

As he was being led from the field with blood pouring from a cut over the eye Jim had to pass F.S., leaning on his bat at the non-striker's end, and it was Fred who, as ever, had the last word on the matter: 'I think I sized up the situation pretty well, didn't I?' In the interests of historical accuracy it is necessary to make the point that Fred denies some of the detail of this story, but who is going to accept his account, rather than Jim's, when it is such a beauty in the Laker version? That was one tour which cannot be remembered with unequivocal pleasure, personal discomfort apart, because it involved Tony Lock being called for throwing – the first time it had happened in a Test since 1897–98 – and the family of umpire Burke suffered physical attack after he had given out J.K. Holt junior lbw on 94 in his debut innings, all this in Jamaica. But at least England squared the rubber after being two down with only two played.

Jim's affection for South Africa having been fired by his wartime visit to Durban, he went there in the winter of 1949–50 to fulfil a coaching engagement – but he had to wait until 1956–57 before he returned as an England player in an official touring party. It was, in his own words, 'the worst series of Test matches in which I ever played'. Now the results, on paper, point to a hard-fought and exciting contest, with England winning the first two Tests and South Africa the last two with the middle one drawn, so what was the cause of Jim's disappointment? There seem to have been three main reasons for this: (1) slow wickets and negative cricket; (2) a deterioration in personal relationships between the players on and off the field; (3) a certain disenchantment with some aspects of the South African way of life as seen at close quarters. Let us look at the points one by one. The wickets generally were indeed of the low and slow variety, discouraging in equal measures attacking bowling and strokemaking batting. Faced with these conditions, South Africa gave a lot of work to Trevor Goddard, the left-arm fast-medium bowler who was the main support to the genuinely quick openers, Adcock and Heine. Goddard, who had been noted as a promising schoolboy player by Laker seven years earlier during his coaching winter in South Africa, had brought to a fine art his just short-of-a-length attacking of the leg stump which could tie down all but the best batsmen and even they were going to hesitate to attempt strokes when the ball was not coming onto the bat. In Trevor Bailey, England had just the man to respond in kind to Goddard's methods. He could bowl line-and-length with the best of them and if a line of on or fractionally just outside the leg-stump was called for, T.E. Bailey would be delighted to provide it. The result was that he bowled more overs than anyone else except J.C. Laker in the five-Test series and the difference in output between the off-spinner and the fast-medium man was just 10 deliveries. Only four centuries were registered in the rubber – one by Roy McLean for South Africa and three by England. In a line-up of such accomplished stroke-players as Cowdrey, Compton and May, it was Doug Insole, of Essex, who topped the averages.

Peter Heine, one of the opening bowlers, was a pretty formidable character, wholly aggressive in attitude and application, who seemed to enjoy hitting batsmen as much as shattering the stumps. Bailey, inevitably, became a *bête noire* with his forward defensive stroke and at one point Heine snarled at him, 'I want to hit you, Bailey. I want to hit you over the heart.' It was, Jim recalled, one of the most extraordinary remarks he had ever heard on a cricket field and it must certainly rank as one of the most appalling. He hit Jim a stinging blow on the shoulder and inquired, entirely without solicitude, 'Have I hurt you?' Laker always regretted that on the spur of the moment he could conjure up no better response than, 'I'll hit you over the head with the bloody bat if you do that again.' It rankled with Jim for years that his response was on the same crude and coarse level as the bowler's inquiry. There were, he felt, a hundred different ways in which he could cut 'the bloody Dutchman' down to size more effectively than the one he had, in a quick-tempered reaction, chosen. By responding in kind, Jim felt he had descended to Heine's level of brutish arrogance and that hurt him far more than the crack on the shoulder. In the final Test, on one of the deadest wickets of all, Jim thoroughly enjoyed cover-driving Heine for four, which in turn infuriated the South African. It was, of course, the classic *player*'s response to provocation and it represented a little personal victory. But it didn't quite compensate for what Jim always remembered as a verbal defeat. Or at any rate a non-victory!

Finally, we come to one aspect of the South African way of life which shocked Jim deeply. As we have seen elsewhere in this story, he and Alan Oakman were close friends on that tour in particular and during the party's stay in Cape Town Oakman had borrowed a car to go out for the evening. Driving back to the hotel he knocked down a coloured man who came shooting out of a side-turning on a bicycle without any warning. He lay on the ground with a broken leg and the shaken Oakman was quickly surrounded by a crowd, who were by no means hostile. In fact they ignored the poor chap lying in agony by his battered bike and greeted Alan, 'Hello, Mr Oakman' ... 'Will you sign my book, Mr Oakman?' ... 'You didn't play a good shot today, Mr Oakman.' Finally a police officer arrived and he took no more notice of the injured cyclist than anyone else. Instead he made an instant appraisal of the situation by asking Oakman rhetorically, 'He was drunk, Mr Oakman, wasn't he?' Getting no response to this from the dazed Englishman, he seized on one man in the crowd: 'You live near this nigger — he's always drunk, isn't he?' And on receiving the response of a slow, fearful nod of the head, the custodian of law and order wrapped up the incident and an ambulance was finally called for.

It was an experience which shocked Oakman and clearly left a profound impression on Laker when it was reported to him. He retained the sort of ambivalent attitude to life in South Africa which so many sportsmen who visit that country share; he had little sympathy with theorists at home who are quick to voice opinions about a country they have never visited, and yet he could not accept, any more than the next Briton, the sort of attitude shown by the policeman to the injured cyclist. 'You find', he said, 'you have to adjust your thinking once you get to South Africa.'

It will probably come as a surprise to many people to whom a cruise seems the ultimate in holiday luxury, to learn that Jim felt it was far from ideal to start a winter tour with a long sea journey. The arguments *for* sea travel, as advanced by many players (and captains) who did their touring that way are that it is a considerable aid to building up team spirit to spend weeks together before the playing part of the trip actually begins; that after a long English season, a sea-voyage was an excellent way of getting rid of the tensions of four months of continuous cricket; and that it was a pretty handy way of getting everyone fully fit before they landed in opposition territory.

The argument can work the other way, of course. Facilities on board ship for getting any cricket practice are virtually nil and the modern view is very much in favour of getting 'out in the middle' at the earliest opportunity. Anyone who was not a good sailor was going to have a pretty miserable time of it before he got to Australia or anywhere else and that would not help either physical fitness or morale. And most of all, sea-travel extended the time when players were away from their families and that was likely to be the strongest argument of all against it.

Just the same, modern cricketers must feel very strongly as they jet about countries and continents,.cramming more and more fixtures into already overcrowded itineraries, that the 'old boys' had it a good deal easier and there can be no denying this aspect of it. Travelling from

Bombay or Madras to Dacca or Karachi might well have taken three days in something less than palatial splendour but at least every such journey meant one game fewer in the schedule. Contrast that with England players in the winter of 1987–88 – tearing about India and Pakistan during the World Cup, following this with a tour of Pakistan, a few weeks at home around Christmas, then off to New Zealand with a couple of matches in Australia squeezed into that tour as well. Tours have become more frequent and more congested. While Laker had a natural professional's sympathy for players caught up on the modern treadmill of fixtures he also felt that they should understand the multiplicity of matches had become necessary to generate the finance to pay the quite generous salaries of the 1980s' international. 'The players should be the last to complain,' he said from time to time. But was it not a chicken and egg situation? Test rates of pay were fairly modest until the massive injection of sponsorship money by the Cornhill Insurance company from 1978 onwards. From that point Test Match fees took a tremendous forward leap and tour payments increased correspondingly. Just as prices, once hiked rarely come down as far as the housewife is concerned, so professional cricketers did not expect to see their wages reduced once they had attained a comfortable level.

Gone, in consequence, are the days when Test players were able to accept omission from the international scene philosophically. It is now a major financial disaster to fall from grace (for whatever reason) after a spell at the top for any length of time when a home series of Tests can bring fees and fringe benefits of more than £10,000 and a winter tour can bring income of almost twice that figure. From 29 Tests in England Jim Laker made £2,370 and from five overseas tours another £2,700. Thirteen years with Surrey brought him wages of £10,000 and his Benefit in 1956 earned him another £11,000 – a very good figure for that time. That means that over 13 years, the best off-spinner in the world made a total of £26,070. A mere 21 years after his retirement he saw Jack Simmons, the Lancashire off-spinner who was never even remotely considered for Test selection, add £120,000 to his bank balance in one season from the proceeds of his Benefit alone. Even allowing for the changes in the value of money between 1959 and 1980, that is a quite staggering difference. Resentment on Laker's part would have been very easy to understand.

There was none. He did not begrudge modern players their massively increased earnings because he felt very strongly that he had played his own cricket at a better time and that was something on which one could not put a monetary value. Not all old players have been able to look at the situation with the same equanimity. There is envy amongst some of those who practised their arts 25 and 30 years ago. But not with many of them. Cricket was indeed a friendlier, happier game as enjoyed by the practitioners of the 1950s and 1960s. There was a greater sense of enjoyment by those who played and, inevitably, it communicated itself to those who watched and reported the game. Jim felt strongly that a deterioration in the relationship between players and the media was a reflection of players' attitude to the cricketing public and he deplored it. Was it not bound to happen, I put to him on one occasion in 1983, when the bulk of the money earned by modern players came from sponsors rather than the men and women who came through the gates and paid admission money? Did this not lead directly to players' attitudes that they had no longer a responsibility to the public, not only to play entertaining cricket but to observe decent standards of behaviour?

With a doubtful shake of the head, Jim responded, 'There's no putting the clock back, is there? But I just can't stand this "ungentlemanly conduct", bad manners, dissent – call it what you like. There is just no need for it and no place for it in a game of cricket.'

His last tour was the one he had coveted for the whole of his playing career – to Australia in the winter of 1958–59 and, with hindsight, it was fated to be an unhappy one in many ways for Jim, despite the fact that he was realising his fondest ambition and notwithstanding his success in heading the averages. As we have seen, there was a long and acrimonious dispute with Peter May before Jim finally agreed to make the 1958–59 tour. May would now be his captain in Australia. His resentment of Freddie Brown for his earlier selectorial shortcomings (as Jim saw them) was also a matter of record. Mr Brown was now to be a co-manager of the tour, jointly with Desmond Eagar. On top of all these potentially contentious circumstances came the Australians' deter-mination, as yet unpublicised, to 'get after him' as a bowler and so avenge to some extent their humiliation of 1956. Those who have questioned Laker's courage in tackling quality opposition in unfavourable conditions must surely have at least some doubts about the veracity of their criticism when considering how many factors were against Jim as he set out for Australia on board the *Iberia* in the early autumn of 1958.

The problems started, in Jim's view, at the very first tour party meeting on the voyage when certain policy matters were laid down. Freddie Brown was to handle all press relations on the tour, rather than the captain. On the 1956–57 tour to South Africa, Peter May had had a wretched time with the bat, totalling only 153 runs in 10 Test innings. This left him with the impression, Jim gathered, that he could not do himself justice as a player when he also had to deal with the press and one can understand this. May has ever been a basically shy person, never feeling completely at home and often actually ill-at-ease in handling media conferences right up to his reign as chairman of the England selectors in the eighties. In 1958 he was dealing with an infinitely more dignified and gentlemanly bunch of cricket correspondents than he was to encounter 30 years later, men with a rather different approach to their duties, but he was not happy about it. And the Australian media were something else altogether – uninhibited, brash, caustic and ever ready for a bit of good, old-fashioned Pommie-bashing.

One cannot help feeling, however, that even May at his most diffident would have been a more diplomatic handler of media relations than Freddie Brown at his best but if the tour captain felt his game was likely to suffer then it was obviously right, from his point of view, that these duties should be handled by somebody else. Jim's view, however, was less tolerant:

> However much sympathy one felt for May as captain and leading batsman, the general feeling was that he was shouldering off a responsibility. Hammond, Hutton and Yardley, for example, had dealt with the press and their play had not suffered as a result. From the press point of view the arrangement was never less than a snag and sometimes looked like developing into a disaster. Freddie Brown, to be frank, was not exactly the most diplomatic man to be in contact with the press and leaving aside his personal manner, he was not competent to tell the press a lot that they wanted to know. The press are criticised often enough for dealing in off-the-field gossip [how much more true this has become 30 years on!] but on this tour what happened to the pressman who wanted to find out about happenings on the field? This, nobody could deny, was the business of the press. The man best qualified to answer questions about the cricket – the captain – was not going to say a word for fear of spoiling his batting.

At that same shipboard meeting, the players were warned about contact with the press and reminded of their contracts which specified that interviews with the media were prohibited. Looking back on the scene from 1988, one cannot help marvelling at this excessive caution in 1958. Even in those far-off days there would be the occasional one – perhaps even two – of the accompanying party of journalists who would take a more sensational line of reporting because there would be one, perhaps two, newspapers whose editorial policy demanded this approach. But there was a complete absence of the 'Number Twos', the second-string reporters whose job it now is to gather 'quotes', to ferret out any aspect of a day's play which will provide an eye-catching headline whether it concerns the day's cricket or an event in the essentially off-duty life of a player. This journalistic scavenging seemed to have reached its low-point during the 1986–7 tour to the West Indies, only to be surpassed in June, 1988, when it resulted in the downfall of Mike Gatting as the England captain – an occasion which one could only see as an utter tragedy, not only for English cricket but for British journalism.

Such developments could not be foreseen in 1958 – and would have been regarded as unthinkable by players and journalists alike – and Jim regarded the dictum of 'not talking to the press' as just plain silly. The tourists knew most of the national and provincial newspaper correspondents as well as they knew their next-door neighbour; they were to be shipboard companions for the next few weeks and after that would be travelling to and fro across Australia in their company, living in the same hotels, exchanging a drink or two in the evening. Was all this to be accomplished with no conversational exchanges beyond a discussion on the weather? It was not a particularly good opening gambit on the part of the tour management.

Next – at this same first team-meeting of the tour – came the devastating announcement that meetings of the Saturday Night Club were to be of no more than one hour's duration and liquid refreshment would consist of nothing more potent than beer! Now the Saturday Night Club was a time-honoured institution on tour. Indeed, while not being organised on the same formal lines, it was an institution at home on the county championship circuit. There was no Sunday League so there was no packing of kit at close of play on Saturday and dashing from Canterbury to Middlesbrough, or Manchester to Swansea. Sunday was golf day or, for the few non-golfers, it was a day for total relaxation. Consequently, Saturday night was letting-the-hair-down night. Not too many players have successfully batted, bowled or fielded with a raging hangover and simple professionalism demanded that mid-week partying was rarely part of the scene. Saturday night, therefore, with no cricket the following day was very definitely Saturday night. On tour – again before the days of Sunday play – it was a very personal hour or two for tourists with many time-honoured traditions: 'courts', fines, forfeits, penances, a song or two, a drink or two. In short, it was fun time, relaxation time and often a major contributory factor in maintaining tour morale and team-spirit. To have this restricted to one hour was bad enough; to be told that they could drink only beer was a bit too much for some of the more seasoned tourists – and remember that Jim Laker, 36 years old, five years of wartime service behind him, a professional cricketer for 12 seasons and man on his fifth overseas tour, was not the sort of chap who took kindly to being treated like a wayward child. His contempt for the thinking behind the new tour regulations was enhanced at the very first meeting of the Saturday Night Club. Freddie Brown drank whisky!

Jim then fell foul of the press in a very personal way. He had already decided to retire from the game at the end of the 1959 season because of increasing problems with his spinning finger which had developed an arthritic condition. It was clearly going to be impossible to carry on much longer and Laker, ever a methodical planner, regarded it as logical to give a year's notice (so to speak) of his intentions. It would give Surrey a full 12 months to think about a possible replacement; it would give Jim a similar period to consider his future (which at that time certainly didn't involve any thoughts of broadcasting or writing about the game); and, reasonably enough, the announcement would provide a bit of window-dressing if any prospective employers in industry, commerce or anywhere else happened to be looking round for a notable sporting personality to take onto the ration-strength. To avoid an incessant knocking on the door of his home by journalists requiring a follow-up story he delayed the announcement until he was on board ship. And since he regarded the calling of a press conference as being a bit over the top he simply slipped the story to a news agency reporter accompanying the tour, knowing that in this way it would reach all newspapers simultaneously. What he did not bargain for was the reaction of individual sports editors back in England when the agency story dropped on their respective desks. Sending a representative to cover a cricket tour is quite an expensive business. Here was the first 'story' of any kind to come from the tour and it had arrived by way of a news agency; the sports editors were not happy. And they voiced their displeasure in a spate of cables from Fleet Street to the *Iberia*. Tour correspondents do not like receiving 'snarls' from their offices and to find it happening almost before the tour had got under way did not please them at all. With hindsight, the only way of keeping them reasonably happy would have been to hold the press conference which Jim felt would be altogether too pompous. And if he had tried to do so, what of the management edict about making statements to the press? It was a tricky one and Jim felt that it resulted in his getting a bad press on the tour. Journalists he had regarded as friends now cut him dead, it seemed. Dark hints appeared in articles which suggested he was quitting because he had got all he could out of the game.

Most of the correspondents on that tour steadfastly denied the claims afterwards but there is no doubt that from that uneasy situation on board ship originated one strand of the allegations that J. C. Laker was a player who carried a chip on his shoulder. Another strand led back to the time of his non-selection for Tests when his qualifications were higher than all others for Jim was never reticent when it came to expressing his views. Thus, while there were players who felt that Jim had 'had a chip' (ignoring, perhaps, his legitimate claims for selection) over the previous eight years, the opinion was now reinforced by that of a squad of newspaper men, too.

Australia won the First and Second Tests in Brisbane and Melbourne, on both occasions by eight wickets, and the Third, in Sydney, was drawn and so the remaining two matches had to be won if England were to retain the Ashes. Fifty-three overs in Sydney had caused the condition of Laker's spinning finger to deteriorate to the point where he could bend it no more than 30 degrees from straight. In short, he could not grip the ball, let alone bowl with it. From a discussion with Peter May about this came the decision that Jim's participation in the Adelaide Test would depend upon an improvement in this condition. After a net in Adelaide he reluctantly told May he 'didn't think he could play'. May, hoping against hope that things might improve, suggested they make no absolute decision until just before the Test started and so, after a meeting between the captain, Freddie Brown and Laker himself, 12 names were announced and the understanding was that Tyson would play if Jim could not. At the eve-of-match press conference the 12 names were announced by Brown and the question-and-answer session began:

'Who will you leave out – a batsman or a bowler?'
'A bowler.'
'Will it be a slow bowler or a fast bowler?'
'We shall decide when we see the wicket.'

Listening to this, Laker did not consider that the manager, perhaps, was playing a cat-and-mouse game and declining to give any potentially helpful information to the opposition until the last possible minute – until, in fact, the Australians had had to decide on the composition of their own team. As Jim saw it (or *heard* it) it was going to appear on the morrow as if he was not playing for reasons other than the genuine one. He didn't like half-truths. But from Brown's point of view and, I am sure, the captain's as well, it would not be good policy to let the Australians know in advance that Laker's injured finger was in a very serious condition. If, by chance, Jim could play the following day, the Aussies would know that, at best, it was a doubtful selection and he might not get through the whole match.

After the next question-and-answer Laker took the unprecedented step of trying to intervene in the manager's press conference, not surprisingly without success.

'Is Laker fully fit to play?'
'He's in the 12, isn't he?'

J. C. did not like this at all. But he liked it even less when, next morning, he told the manager and captain he was definitely not fit and Brown went to the press box to announce: 'Laker has just come along and said his finger is not fit for him to play.'

Whatever sympathy one has with the manager on his efforts to gain a tactical advantage over the opposition on the evening before the Test, this announcement to the press as recalled afterwards by Laker has to be seen as horribly and unjustifiably damaging to the bowler. It resulted in a critical press for J. C. L. based essentially on the late announcement and coloured by the manager's form of words. It led to claims that, 'Laker should have played despite the injury because this was the vital Test. It was his duty to play no matter what happened to the finger afterwards.' And Laker's response to that was as follows:

> If there had been any logic in these arguments I would have done my damnedest to play. If I had thought I could do anything to help England win the match, no thought of the future would have stopped me. But I knew the truth; had I played I would have been letting down England who most likely would have been landed with a useless passenger. My decision wasn't easy, for I wanted to play; but I feel I took the most honest and correct course and no amount of malicious and ill-informed mud-slinging can alter the view.

Patriotic and sentimental flag-waving would always seem nonsense to Jim Laker when ranged alongside cold logic and in this instance at any rate his attitude was justified: Godfrey Evans soldiered on behind the stumps even though he went into the game with a broken finger.

He scored four and none and Tom Graveney had to take over as wicketkeeper. The genial Godfrey might have captured the heroic headlines but Jim Laker felt he had scored the points for commonsense.

One way and another, this sounds to have been a rather miserable tour for Laker, especially after his disappointments in missing two previous trips to Australia and taking into account his burning desire to play in that country. And yet it was not all disaster. The spinning finger — after its rest in Adelaide — had recovered sufficiently for Jim to bowl in the last Test, enabled him to bowl more overs (127.6 — eight-ball overs in those days) and to take more wickets (15) at a better average (21.20) than anyone else in the Tests. He brought back some amusing memories like George Duckworth organising hordes of porters and fleets of taxis in Bombay 'with the air of a prince', Godfrey Evans riding an elephant in Ceylon (as it then was) as if it were the usual form of transport at home in Kent, the boyish Roy Swetman (second wicketkeeper on the tour) being mistaken for *the son* of one of the tourists; the occasional Fred Trueman epigram and the party's over-dressed attendance at a theatrical performance of 'Ladies' Night in a Turkish Bath' in Perth. But, as ever, one of his most treasured memories was of Peter Richardson cocking a characteristic snook at authority while the *Iberia* was in equatorial reaches. After being rebuked by the manager for arriving at breakfast without a tie, Richardson returned wearing not only a necktie but an overcoat and scarf as well! Only P. E. Richardson would have been prepared to break his fast in sweltering heat in order to make his point.

While his visit to New Zealand, back in 1951, was not a tour in the accepted sense, Jim enjoyed the tranquil life-style of the country without in any way relaxing the firm views he held on certain aspects of the game of cricket. It is interesting to look back nearly 40 years at the advice he gave to the Auckland squad he coached as they were setting out for the first two games of the Plunket Shield season:

> Many very good top-class cricketers have failed to make the grade in representative or international cricket, not because they were not sufficiently good as cricketers but because they lacked the vital thing in a cricketer's make-up. I mean temperament.
>
> I believe that if one is endowed with reasonably steady nerves, is capable of 100 per cent concentration and has a fair share of courage, one can master temperament. To young batsmen going into senior representative cricket I would offer this advice: You have been selected

because the ability is there. Therefore go in to bat believing you are going to make runs. Take guard, get your head down and concentrate for all you are worth. If by chance you are beaten all ends up in the first over, remember the thoughts of the great Herbert Sutcliffe. Whenever he had such an experience he always said to himself, 'Thank goodness that's over. He can't possibly bowl another one as good as that.'

I would urge the young also to remember that they will be batting on wickets which may be a little strange. As a consequence it is desirable to persuade oneself to have a look at the ball and to become accustomed to the pace of the wicket before trying delicate cuts and hooks. The bowling will be more accurate and better directed than in Saturday afternoon cricket and to counter this the batsman must be looking for sharply-run singles. He must also be trying to make ones into twos. A most important feature to remember is that while 30 or 40 is a useful Saturday afternoon contribution, it means a failure in four-day cricket. By the time one has reached the thirties, one should be well set and have laid the foundation for a big score. Then it is necessary to keep one's head, to carry on playing shots and at all costs to avoid throwing one's wicket away.

Bowlers promoted to representative cricket will, like the batsmen, have a far more difficult job than before. Not only will the batsmen be much better players but the wickets will be better than bowlers have previously experienced. The first essential of representative bowling must, therefore, be accuracy. On top of accuracy, a bowler must be able to introduce some of the intricacies of a bowler's art — flight and pace variation which are often not necessary in club games.

Perhaps the most noticeable difference between club and representative cricket is to be seen in ground fielding, catching and placing of fields. Concentration in the field must be 100 per cent and everyone must be alert to snap up the chances which invariably win matches. Catches always have been, and always will be, missed by every cricketer. But, whereas no one drops them on purpose, the number, by practice and concentration, can be kept to a minimum. It is probable that in representative cricket one will spend a couple of days in the field. To give of one's best for the whole time, one must be really fit. And so for young players I would strongly recommend some serious training. Instead of spending two hours in a net, it would have more point if one spent an hour in the net and the other hour doing physical training or half a dozen laps of the field. In England I play six and often seven days of cricket a week. I know from experience that it took my body some time to become accustomed to the strain after I left Saturday afternoon cricket and became a full-time professional. Added to the mere physical demand is the atmosphere, the tenseness and the keenness of representative cricket. I have always found that bowling 20 overs in a Test Match is equivalent to 40 overs in an everyday county game.

In some ways that exhortation by Jim Laker in 1950 shows him to have been ahead of his time and if many of his other points are regarded as basics they are most certainly as true in 1989 as they were nearly 40 years earlier – and in some cases they seem to have been forgotten. It would not be a bad thing at all if that advice was posted in every school and youth team dressing-room throughout this country.

JOURNALIST
AND
COMMENTATOR

There is a tremendous tragic irony in the fact that Jim Laker had commentated on just 111 Tests when he died — 111 or the 'Nelson', is of course the major numerical superstition amongst first-class cricketers, or at least amongst batsmen. It is stronger in some than others. Few players, or ex-players, are quite as ostentatious in their observation of the 'Nelson' as David Shepherd, the former Gloucestershire batsman who became one of the best umpires in the world. Whenever 111 (or multiples of it) appears on the scoreboard he hops from one leg to the other in a state of some agitation. In the 1987 season he was officiating when a total reached 444 at which point I seem to remember there was a substantial delay in proceedings and 'Shep's' reaction rivalled that of a whirling dervish with St Vitus' Dance. I like to think Jim enjoyed, somewhere, the humour of it all; certainly it would bring that grim, sardonic smile to his lips.

After his start at a Cavaliers' match at Cambridge he 'graduated' to Test Match commentary at Edgbaston in June, 1971 — the First Test against Pakistan when another debutant was a slim, handsome young man called Imran Khan. It was the game in which Zaheer Abbas scored 274, Mushtaq Mohammad 100 and Asif Iqbal 104 not out and England followed on for the first time against Pakistan. In the 110 Tests that followed I cannot recall Jim ever altered his style or in any way changed in personality. It is difficult even to say that his confidence grew as his broadcasting career developed because Jim was perfectly confident from the start. He had been asked to talk about cricket; he knew cricket, so he was simply talking about something he was well qualified to discuss. He may well have refined his technique over the years and we shall look at that aspect with men (and one woman) who worked with him more than I did. One thing is quite clear: he very quickly established his authority as a specialist observer of the game so that in 1975 Ken Lawrence, then Sports Editor of the *Daily Express*, decided that the authority Laker brought to comments on the game was something he wanted to include in the cricket coverage of his newspaper.

He approached Jim, who accepted the invitation to write for the *Express* and Pat Gibson (then number two to the cricket correspondent, Crawford White) was given the job of 'ghosting' the Laker comments. It was the start of an association which Pat, and the Laker family, remember with affection. Yet the professional journalist must have approached his role with a certain diffidence. My own impression of Jim was that he never really accepted that men who had not played the game at his level had any right to be talking or writing about those who had. He would shrug his shoulders and reply, 'So what?' to any suggestion that this view was a little extreme.

It was an attitude of which Pat Gibson was aware. 'I had heard about his tendency towards intolerance,' he recalls,

> I knew his reputation as a dour Yorkshireman and I knew he would not suffer fools gladly. I am delighted to say that from the moment I first met him we never had a wrong word and I became very fond of Jim. At first I was flattered to think he thought I knew a little bit about the game. I certainly knew a great deal more after 10 years association with him. We became pretty close and in due course we became family friends. He was, of course, a different man with his family from the rather abrasive character he could be at times to the outside world. I had stayed on for a holiday in the West Indies with my wife after the winter tour of 1985–86 when I got a cable from the office saying Jim was seriously ill and asking me to prepare an obituary. It was the saddest – and perhaps the hardest – job I have had to do as a newspaperman.

I put to Gibson my theory that if Jim had actually played for Yorkshire, instead of Surrey, he would not have been as sympathetic to the Boycott cause as he was in a very public way. Pat pondered this for a moment, then offered the view: 'Boycott respected Jim, asked for his advice. Jim thought he could help in what was obviously a dreadful situation in Yorkshire. He badly wanted to help sort it out.'

And how difficult was it to 'ghost' a man as fiercely opinionated as J. C. Laker who, if he believed he was right, would defend his viewpoint to the death? Says Gibson:

> He didn't really need a ghost. He was perfectly able to write his own copy from the start. My role was really to apply an *Express*-type intro and perhaps adjust an odd phrase or two to conform with the paper's style. But in the matter of writing about cricket, Jim Laker needed nobody's help. His very first piece, from Edgbaston in 1975, was to condemn the decision to put Australia in to bat. He did that before a ball was bowled and, as the world knows, Australia won by an innings and 85 runs. It cost Mike Denness the England captaincy.

Laker's aptitude for journalism found further expression when, in the winter of 1978–79, the first issue of the new magazine *Wisden Cricket Monthly* was being prepared and he accepted an invitation to join the editorial board. He displayed a quite un-Laker-like emotion, Editor David

Frith remembers, by expressing the view that the project was 'quite exciting'. Afterwards this little excess became a private joke between the two of them. Frith understood Jim better than most; he attributes that occasionally aggressive front he presented to the world to a basic shyness, and clearly he had a great affection for the man.

Jim wrote on a wide variety of topics for *Wisden Cricket Monthly* and his editor recalls that his copy, written to length and neatly typed (thank you, Lilly?) was always delivered right on time. 'At least once over the seven-year period of their association Jim sent a postcard with his rate of pay aligned with the current rate of inflation and never let the magazine overlook the importance of matching his output with the proper reward.' That comment from David Frith, one of the outstanding cricket journalists of his day, indicates why the two of them were very much on the same wavelength as far as humour was concerned. He follows it with this tribute:

I cherished the time when Jim had just finished his television stint at Lord's and would sidle silently through the press box doorway, hands thrust deeply into his trouser pockets. There would be a wink and he'd shuffle over and sit down. We'd talk for a while, sometimes about the magazine, more often about things in general. Golden moments. I called to see him after his operation (an aenorism of the aorta, in 1981) and was shocked at the shrunken, grey figure sitting in a dressing gown in the corner of the bedroom in Putney. He had lost stones in weight. He showed me his scar, from collar-bone down to lower abdomen and I had to sit down. My legs simply went. I didn't stay all that long. Lilly was anxious he should not overdo it. In a weak voice he talked about this and that and I remember how he chuckled as he described how the burglars had taken his 1956 mementos – all except the silver salver which hung on the wall (now safely stored in a bank vault) and which the evil cretins must have mistaken for a mirror as they shone their torches on it. It was marvellous to see him pick up after that as it was to hear the tremendous ovation when he made the Man of the Match presentation at Old Trafford after his come-back.

Wouldn't you agree that a lifelong shyness was perhaps *the* outstanding characteristic? He supported WCM activities, attending various functions but always seeming so passive as to give the impression he was under personal siege. I never ceased to marvel how he, of all people, could rise to his feet and address a vast audience with considerable (apparent) confidence. I have known no more choking funerals than Jim's and Ken Barrington's. Great blokes, both.

Jim remained implacably and immovably Yorkshire in at least one aspect of his commentary life – his refusal to change by even one cadence or syllable his natural style of speaking. Listener-viewers wrote to newspapers in positive anguish at his dropping of certain hard consonants, notably the final letter 'g' as in 'battin'' and 'bowlin''. He was as unmoved by such criticisms as Richie Benaud would have been by critical references to his Australian accent. Richie, in fact, regarded those complaints directed at Jim as 'trite'; Jim himself regarded them as very close to an impertinence. He had been hired, as he saw it, to provide expert comments to accompany the television picture based on his knowledge and experience of the game. He should not be expected to sound like Laurence Olivier (or even Ted Dexter) because that was not what he was about. The tone and terms he employed were of considerably less importance than the content of what he had to say. It is a tradition which has been followed by colleagues like Ray Illingworth (who drops initial aitches as regularly as Jim neglected final gees) and Tom Graveney (who splits infinitives without regret).

Is there an argument for the critics? Perhaps, 30 or 40 years ago, they might have found some sympathy in the higher echelons of the BBC when the Corporation's use of the spoken word was a model for the English-speaking world. But no longer – surely? – in an era when an endless stream of ungrammatical sentences pour from our loudspeakers: 'The Government *has* decided that *their* policy', etc. and when the Director General of the BBC, no less, publicly regales us with the Americanisations of 'hopefully' and 'presently' in contexts for which the words were not originally intended. Perhaps it can come as only a minor surprise to see the inhabitants of Belgium described in the *Daily Mail* (and in a headline, too!) as 'Belgiums'. So is it fair criticism to object to imperfections in the pronunciation of men whose job it simply is to provide expert comments; to utter a minimum of words which are designed to improve the viewers' understanding of what is happening on their screens? Of course not.

There was, however, criticism, too, of the strict economy of words exercised by both Jim and Richie. 'Talk more', pleaded a number of viewers. 'Why the long silences?'

This is an interesting point because the cardinal rule of television commentary must always be: 'Don't insult the intelligence of the viewers by telling them exactly what they can already see happening on their screen.' Benaud's views, therefore, are very important:

I learned quite a bit from Jim on economy of words. He may have learned something from me but it was a good combination. I was also influenced by Phil Lewis who started off with cricket commentaries, then by David Kenning and Nick Hunter who produced later. The other man I have learned from is David Hill, the Channel 9 producer in Australia. He has a marvellous grasp of what, and how much, people should say. He believes the greatest weapon on television is silence and he's quite right. People write to me (as they did to Jim) and say, 'Will you please say more?' and I take it to mean we have got it about right. If there is something to add to the picture on the screen I will add to it, as Jim would do also.

It is difficult to quarrel with any of that and I am bound to say that as a radio commentator whose discipline it is to keep talking all the time I was lost in admiration of the way the Benaud and Laker combination contrived to say so much in so few words; I shall come to an illustration of this shortly. But not all correspondents who write to commentators are caustic in their criticism by any means. Most try to be helpful if, in fact, they have anything to criticise; others like to poke a little, gentle fun, without malice.

There was, it seems to me, a great deal of affection in the trouble Mr Jack Cookson, of Walsall, took in writing a series of verses called 'Negative "G"' or 'Jim Laker's Lament', which he sent to Peter West during the 1976 series against the West Indies.

'The great day is dawnin'
For durin' the mornin'
The quest for the Ashes will start
With Jim commentatin'
And teams concentratin'
The nation's at least in good heart.

The English first innin's
From slow, sure beginnin's
Is takin' a turn for the worse
The wickets are tumblin'
Supporters are grumblin'
The captain should be in a hearse.

How brittle our battin'
On grass or on mattin'
Tail-enders to rescue — take heart
Why not send for Virgin
He'll need little urgin'
To tear the quick bowlers apart.

What with Roberts and Holdin'
And Holder, their bowlin'
Is more than we English can stand.
Excuses aren't heeded
No alibis needed
We're bein' emphatically tanned.'

If we grant Mr Cookson a little licence for his use of the term 'Ashes' in an England v West Indies series and explain that Roy Virgin was a Northamptonshire (and former Somerset) batsman, it adds up to an engaging little comment on the Laker commentary style.

A certain pedantry has always been present in my own (radio) style of commentary and this was a source of some amusement to Jim, bearing in mind that we had been born less than nine miles from each other and in roughly the same period. He ribbed me about what we called my 'correspondence course accent' and affected not to understand why I regarded grammatical exactitude (or as close as I could get to it) as vitally important. Being trained in newspaper journalism at a time when one was schooled in such matters as the necessity for getting one's grammar, spelling and punctuation right (sadly, no longer the case), I regarded it as only logical to translate this into terms of the spoken word as well when I turned to broadcasting. I had long since decided that a little tidying up of the slovenliness of my natural West Riding speech was necessary to make myself generally understood, in any case, and so I first approached the microphone as a vocal hybrid. I was not a great Test cricketer whose expert comments could embellish a television picture irrespective of how the words were uttered; it was my job to give the facts but to paint a picture and set a scene as well — and *not* to allow silences to develop.

So Jim and I — two Yorkshire lads from the same area and similar backgrounds — worked alongside each other for many years employing entirely different approaches to basically the same job: describing events at a cricket match. This often gave Jim a great deal of fun but none greater than my story of the terrors of golf commentary, to which I switched once or twice each summer and in particular to the Open Championship. No matter how strictly one disciplines oneself in speech there are certain pitfalls which inspire utter dread and in the case of the West Riding man the worst of these by far has to be two similar vowel-sounds requiring different enunciation but which occur in proximity to each other. The nightmare for me was 'foot' and 'putt'.

Originally, I commentated on events on the putting green in a state of abject terror, dreading the moment when 'putt' would come out either as 'pat' or the most gutteral 'pu.u.u.tt'. The dangers of this happening were all especially enhanced when 'putt' followed the word 'foot'. My natural form of speech, from birth, childhood and adolescence in deepest West Yorkshire, cried out to express itself with 'pu.u.u.t' while the self-taught elocution demanded something much closer to an over-the-top 'pat'. Writing a script and reading it to a studio microphone was one thing; ad-libbing, describing this vital part of a golf round as it happened was altogether different.

To add to the dangers of this verbal minefield, there was the necessity (in describing a putt) of keeping the voice down to an absolute minimum, because while I would be operating within a few yards of the player it was vital that I should not be audible to him and provide a distraction. When a golfer is putting in the last round of the Open a single stroke can make a difference of £10,000 or more in prize-money, or, taking the longer view, £1 million or more if that stroke means the difference between winning and losing the championship. As the father of a professional golfer who was quite frequently playing in the championship I was describing I was doubly aware of the need to be unobtrusive and so, even on the coldest day, I have crouched beside greens at St Andrews and Muirfield, Lytham and Birkdale, perspiring with fear of (a) being heard by the listeners in a vocal gaucherie and (b) being heard at all by a competitor. Looking back on those days I often wonder how I managed any description of play at all.

The answer, of course, was to limit the possibility of error and, with a mixture of cowardice and circumspection, I banished the phrase 'four foot putt' from my golf-commentating vocabulary and took refuge in the infinitely safer 'four-footer'. It was after returning from one Open in the seventies that I discussed these fears with Jim and he affected a certain incredulousness. 'Why get hot and bothered?' he asked. 'Just call it as you see it and don't concern yourself about how it sounds.' It was, alas, an over-simplification. If it had been Dai Rees (that wonderful former

Ryder Cup captain who often accompanied me on those final rounds of the Open to provide expert comments) it would not have mattered how *he* sounded; it was his golf expertise that the listener was waiting for – what club was going to be used, how the player would shape his shot, what would be the consequences of a dropped stroke at a particular hole.

I never really decided whether Jim was serious or not in pouring scorn on such fears of mine. We often returned to the topic and, as a highly intelligent man who had become an accomplished professional broad-caster, he must have known that a cricket commentator who sounded as though he had stepped straight out of the pages of a J. B. Priestley comedy would never have got within a thousand miles of Test Match Special. Keighley Boys' Grammar School taught me much for which I have always been grateful but a delicate handling of the vowel-sound 'u' was, unfortunately not in the curriculum.

Gradually I found myself inclining to the view that Jim did, in fact, understand the problem and was simply indulging in a favourite pastime of stirring something up. There was a simple riposte to this. I had only to mention the number of people who wrote to us – far more letters are addressed by listeners to the Test Match Special radio commentary team than the television team receive in their box – saying they watched the television pictures with the commentary turned down and listened simultaneously to the radio commentary, to goad him to a mighty fury. 'That's just plain daft', he would fume – and the sentiments are echoed today by Richie Benaud.

'That is something which Jim and I were as one on', he says, most emphatically. 'We couldn't understand why anyone could turn the sound down and listen to someone talking about something which bore no relevance to the picture.' (While listeners write to us, the radio box, telling us this with the intention of paying a compliment, there are those who write to the television commentators telling them with a view to being insulting.) And while it would be true that for most of the time the television picture would indeed be showing something other than what we are talking about in the radio box I think it is necessary to say that at the moment the ball is being delivered, the radio commentary is very much about what the television picture is showing. Having said that, Richie is quite right, of course; it does seem largely illogical. But in the TMS box we don't knock people who write on those lines; we are obliged to them and flattered by their support! As a means of side-tracking Jim Laker, however, when he was in full-cry as a critic of my 'correspondence-course' accent, the topic was a godsend.

In the late seventies, when John Arlott began to scale down his broadcasting commitments on both sides of cricket coverage, television and radio, he started by discarding commentary on the John Player (Sunday) League and Jim asked me how I felt about joining him by taking over from John. I was startled by the approach. As a BBC producer first, and commentator second, I knew perfectly well that the job was not in Jim's gift, so to speak. It would be David Kenning, the television cricket producer, who would make the decision on who succeeded John. On the other hand I knew that Jim wielded a great deal of influence at that time and was very close to Kenning. It so happened that David was a close friend of mine, too, as we had worked together for a time in Manchester and spent a lot of social hours together. So I quietly mentioned to him that Jim had approached me and he replied, 'That's right. How about it?'

It needed a good deal of thought. Two Yorkshiremen working together in the same commentary box? One could foresee a lot of letters to the press if that came about. 'Disgusted, Tunbridge Wells', would have a field day. There were a lot of other things against the idea as well. I had never made-any secret of the fact that I detested the Sunday afternoon circus in which batsmen prostituted their own artistry and bowlers were simply cannon-fodder — or perhaps camera-fodder was a more appropriate term since the John Player League, as I saw it, was designed as a cheap and convenient bit of television for BBC 2 to fill four-and-a-half hours of Sunday afternoon, as it originally did, and a boost for county treasurers because the crash-bang-wallop of 40-overs-a-side brought people into grounds who were never otherwise seen there. My masters in BBC Radio knew and accepted my position on the Sunday League and never asked me to go to one of those games. How would it now look if I said I was going to cover them for television?

I weighed up the other arguments against making the move. I had now been broadcasting on radio for 25 years, first as a freelance, then on the BBC staff. I had dabbled very rarely indeed in television and in all truth I was a bit afraid of the medium. Could I hope to make the transition with any hope of success? As for following the Arlott act — that was impossible. Just as I have always regarded Brian Johnston as the best natural broadcaster I have ever known, John was most certainly the best descriptive artist in my broadcasting world. There was no possibility of my being able to replace John; it was, perhaps, possible simply to follow him and see if my personal style was acceptable to the viewers. The matter was partly resolved when John told David Kenning that he would rather not make the long trip from a Test at Old Trafford on the Sunday rest day to cover a John Player League game at Southampton. 'Now's the chance,' said Laker. 'Have a go at this one and let's see how it turns out.'

In the end it was the challenge of tackling something completely different which decided me and on the Saturday night of the Test Jim and I drove to London, spent a very pleasant evening at his home in Putney, and drove on to Southampton through the coast-bound traffic on a beautifully sunny Sunday morning. The game was Hampshire v Lancashire and I remember being on the microphone when Clive Lloyd scored the fastest televised 50. Did I talk too much?

My chief recollection of the game was the disappointment of seeing Barry Richards get out cheaply, because there was no one in the country better to watch than the brilliant South African in full cry but it all seemed to go reasonably well. However, I felt no burning desire to make television commentary my life's work, even if anyone asked me to do so. Radio was very much my first love and I most certainly had no intention of giving it up. But the occasional bit of television . . .? Perhaps.

By now the word had got around that Arlott was giving up Sunday television commentary after that season and a dozen candidates or more were lining up, anxious — desperately so in some cases — to be given a chance to succeed him. Some, understandably, strongly resented that the favourite for the role seemed to be a man who was already established as a radio commentary regular and, moreover, held a nice, secure post as Senior Outside Broadcasts Producer in the north. There is something about the in-fighting which goes on in television which brings out the very worst in human nature and I began to feel the knives going into my back. I was not at all happy and mentioned this to Jim. He laughed and urged me, with admirable succinctness, to forget the carpers (or words to that effect!). And he followed this up by asking how I would like to work with him on a Gillette Cup semi-final. This created problems because I would be required by radio for that game but, as always happens in any tug-of-war between the two broadcasting agencies, television won hands down and so came my salutary experience at Taunton.

On 16 August, 1978, therefore, Somerset were at home to Essex in one of the Gillette Cup semi-finals and Viv Richards started on his way to a brilliant 116 by crashing a flurry of fours from the first few balls he received. Sitting in the passenger seat, so to speak, all my radio commentator's instincts cried out for a description of this strokeplay.

Words, phrases, formed in my mind and pleaded to be uttered into the microphone which Jim Laker held – silently. When the fourth four in rapid succession raced to the boundary, he finally spoke: 'He doesn't hang about, this chap.' The words were uttered with a little smile and they seemed to be addressed as much to the other two people in the box (the scorer and myself) as to the world at large. In that moment I understood, really for the first time, the essential difference between radio and television commentary. Viewers could see for themselves what was taking place out in the middle; they did not need any embellishment. But what was almost an aside – 'He doesn't hang about' – would sum up what most viewers were thinking at that moment. It was, in fact, a thought, spoken aloud – rather than a professional observation – and it was couched in terms with which just about everyone could identify. People's form of words might differ but as a natural reaction, Jim had captured the moment. In its very simplicity, it constituted brilliant television commentary and easy though that may sound, very few people can achieve it.

Compare this with much of modern commentary on cricket; compare it with Australian television commentary, with British soccer commentary, with American golf commentary. In each of these there seems to be a compulsion on the part of the commentators to keep talking in a way which can be, and often is, infuriating to the viewers who naturally resent being told about what they can see perfectly well is taking place. Richie Benaud has the gift; Jim Laker had it; Peter Alliss has it at golf, just as Henry Longhurst had. If you are going to say something on television, make it something worthwhile, something which adds to the picture, something with which the viewers can identify in their own mind or which enhances their understanding of what is happening.

Before the end of that day at Taunton, Jim enjoyed a particularly Laker-like joke. I had noticed, and been intrigued by, the rota of commentary periods which meant that I would be talking through the final stages of the game. This was something more than unusual – the expert leaving the climax to the novice. And the game was heading towards a dizzy finish. With half an hour or so remaining, Jim stood up and said, lazily, 'Right. It seems to be building up nicely for you. I'll leave you to it.' Nervously – and I was damned nervous – I quavered, 'Where are you going?' The last thing I wanted was to be left alone with the commentary as the game reached boiling point. There is a great comfort in knowing someone else is there, a second opinion if you like, to confirm or correct a diagnosis. To be left on my own induced something very

LEFT It's only Lucozade...Jim
after taking 6 for 55 against
Australia at Headingley, 1956
(Sport & General)

BELOW J. C. the batsman...43
against the Australians at The
Oval in 1956 after taking all 10
for 88 (Keystone)

LEFT Old Trafford, 1956. 'Won't this rain ever stop?'
(Y.E. News)

RIGHT The rain has stopped. Now will the sun come out? Jim with Peter May on the Old Trafford balcony, July, 1956
(Sport & General)

ABOVE Family outing. Father carries Angela (aged two) to the car. Fiona, a year older, can do it alone (*Keystone*)

RIGHT No pitch invasions. No dancing about and punching the air. A slightly embarrassed Laker leads England in after routing the Aussies at Old Trafford in 1956 (*Sport & General*)

A couple of souvenirs of Old Trafford, 1956. A month later, at The
Oval, Lancashire chairman Tommy Burrows presents the 9 for 37
and 10 for 53 cricket balls to Jim while Stuart Surridge looks on
(*Keystone*)

All pals together – for the moment. Jim with Roy Gilchrist and
Everton Weekes before the start of the 1957 West Indies tour of
England (*Sport & General*)

RIGHT That high action is seen,
round the wicket, at the Oval's
Vauxhall end. The gas-holders
have seen it all before *(Keystone)*

BELOW Jim and Brian Johnston help with a Charity Tombola, Park
Lane Hotel, 1957 *(Keystone)*

MCC in Australia, 1958-59: Back row, left to right: D. Montague, Arthur Milton, Willie Watson, Peter Richardson, Roy Swetman, George Duckworth; middle row: Tony Lock, Brian Statham, Peter Loader, Raman Subba Row, Tom Graveney, Frank Tyson, Freddie Trueman; front row: Freddie Brown, Trevor Bailey, Colin Cowdrey, Peter May, Godfrey Evans, Jim Laker, Desmond Eagar *(Topham)*

The spin twins, Laker and Lock, have their tickets checked at St Pancras Station, on their way to Australia in 1958 *(Topham)*

'It's only the truth. What is everyone getting so excited about?' Jim with his controversial book, published in 1960 (BBC Hulton)

'So this is the joker who rolled us over in 1956?' Crowds at the Waca gound in Perth watch Jim in the nets on the 1958-59 tour (Topham)

The happy grandfather

Four men who have captained England attend Jim's funeral in 1986:
Tom Graveney, Tony Lewis, Mike Denness and Sir Leonard Hutton
(*Topham*)

close to panic in my mind. But my partner said airily, 'Oh, I'm doing the Man of the Match award. Didn't I tell you?' He then sauntered blithely over to the other side of the ground.

Sure enough it happened. Essex needed three to win off the last ball of the match. John Lever heaved towards mid-wicket and the camera, understandably, was swung round in that direction. But the ball had found the edge of the bat and was trickling, with agonising slowness, down towards deep third-man. Now one of the cardinal rules which had been hammered into me before embarking on television commentary was: 'Don't describe what you can see as you look round the field. Talk about what is on your monitor because that is what the viewers are looking at.' But my monitor now showed a sea of dancing spectators at mid-wicket while the ball was making laboured progress towards third-man. Was it Brian Rose or Peter Roebuck? Identification which would have presented no problem half-an-hour, or even 10 runs, earlier, suddenly became tangled up with a jumbled mass of panic-stricken thoughts. Lever and Neil Smith, meanwhile, were haring up and down the pitch in search of three runs. Had they taken one by this time or were they on the second? Lever had hit the ball and he was coming back; it must be the second. But should I now be talking about what was happening at mid-wicket (nothing, except wild rejoicing) or third-man where the action was? Down my 'cans' I could hear the director screaming at his cameraman to give him a shot of the ball and the fieldsman. A decision had to be made and my brain was refusing to function. I plunged, by this time neither knowing nor caring whether it was the right thing to do or not, into a description of Rose's (or Roebuck's?) race towards the ball and the frenzied Lever-Smith gallop taking place between the stumps. It all seemed to be happening in slow motion as I made one last despairing effort to gather my wits.

As the return arrived in the wicketkeeper's gloves I turned back to the monitor and as long as I live I shall never forget the close-up picture of Neil Smith's expression when he finally hurled himself headlong towards the crease. He looked up at the umpire, Arthur Jepson, pleading with every fibre of his being for the decision to be 'not out'. Had they run two, or three? Smith at the batting crease – it must be three. In that case, if the decision was 'not out', Essex had won by one wicket. But wait a minute – if he was 'out', the scores were level at 287 each. What then? The decision was 'out.' As the umpire's finger was raised, I turned and looked pleadingly around me, begging for confirmation from someone, anyone, of the words which now babbled from my dry mouth

... 'So Somerset, 287 for eight, win by virtue of having lost fewer wickets than Essex, 287 all out.' I sank back with a gasp and a pulse-rate which seemed about 100 per cent above normal.

About 10 light-years later, it seemed, I picked up the 'lazy' microphone on which I had direct contact with the producer and said, guiltily, 'Sorry I abandoned the monitor but it seemed the only thing to do in the circumstances.' 'Right', he replied tersely. I was not to know he was still involved with the erring cameraman and Authority at the Television Centre who wanted to know why they had been given a shot of mid-wicket when the ball was at third-man. Some time after that, as I sat shaking in the Somerset Committee room, J. C. Laker joined me. 'Quite a finish,' he grinned amiably. 'Well done.' And the veteran of more than 30 years in the communications medium felt like a schoolboy who has just been patted on the head by his sports master after scoring a winning try. I didn't think, though, that my nerves would stand up to much more television commentary.

We had one more mid-week adventure after that, another semi-final at Northampton which finished in conditions so dark that the monitor provided just about our only means of seeing what was happening out in the middle and Jim Griffiths played the most notable innings of his career. Big Jim was one of that select band who took more wickets than he scored runs in first-class cricket but his miraculous survival in the gloaming on that occasion scotched a win for Lancashire which had seemed inevitable. Jim (Laker) carried out the last 20 minutes commentary on that occasion and I sat back with a smile and listened to my radio colleagues, Henry Blofeld and Trevor Bailey, operating on the other side of a flimsy curtain, trying to keep up with events they could scarcely see. Henry, however, never panics and in due course the inevitable bus, which he really could see, came to his rescue!

Most, if not all good things come to an end and David Kenning moved on from cricket production to golf. New producers came with whom Jim's influence was not quite so strong — though there remained a bond of professional respect and personal regard between him and all those who directed his operations — producers with their own ideas of new men to be tried. Gracefully, and entirely happily, I returned to radio commentary where I felt more comfortable and distinctly more at home. But it had been an interesting experience and I was glad I had undertaken it.

I did manage a small revenge upon my friend — for Taunton, 1978 — at Edgbaston when a Test Match finished early and we went off to play golf at the very hospitable club about half a mile from the ground. These days, four balls of grim intensity are played at the crack of dawn between Jack Bannister, Tony Lewis, Richie Benaud and Ted Dexter, but ours was a more civilised round undertaken on a sunny afternoon. Jim, off a 16 handicap, was a properly coached player; at that time I was off 14 and very much a self-taught hacker, perversely proud of the fact that I have never had a lesson in my life. Thus I had to give Jim a couple of shots but I beat him two and one in what must have been the most proficient 18 holes I have ever played. The following season, when again an opportunity presented itself I threw out the challenge and received an extremely curt rebuff: 'I've given the game up.' 'Why?' I inquired. 'That game last season finished me off,' replied the competitive Laker in tones of deep self-disgust. 'If a —— like you can beat me, then it's time to pack up.' In point of fact Jim gave up the game because he no longer felt well enough to play, but he wouldn't admit it.

It was at Edgbaston that Jim returned to commentary duty after his illness in 1981. As usual, we enjoyed the splendid hospitality of the Cornhill Insurance sponsors after the first day's play and the even greater pleasure of chatting to old friends in the game but Jim did not want to linger long, so soon after his operation and convalescence, so he drove back with me to the Holiday Inn. Half way up Queensway, *en route* to the pub, is a roundabout with traffic lights and, intending to go straight on, I pulled up in the middle of the three lanes. When the lights showed green I moved forward, only to find the car on my left, driven by a young Chinese chap with his girl friend as a passenger, was turning right! He hit my near-side front wing but never hesitated; he drove straight on, pursued by an extremely angry (and reputedly xenophobic) radio commentator. I managed to overtake him and to force him to stop, then addressed myself to him on the subject of driving in England, suggesting that perhaps pedalling a rickshaw in Hong Kong might be the full extent of his capabilities. He retaliated by quoting at some length the provisions of the Race Relations Act and the discussion continued on a fairly acrimonious note. At length, I extracted a name and address but failed totally to get any details of his insurance cover. Then, turning round in my exasperation, I was alarmed to see Laker slumped over the bonnet of the car, shaking uncontrollably. As I rushed back to him, my Chinese acquaintance made a hurried departure and my temper was not improved by the discovery that Jim was shaking – with uncontrollable laughter! 'It would have to be you he hit, wouldn't it?' he choked. 'A Chinese waiter. Don't they usually get in the left hand lane to turn right?'

And off he went again, almost hysterical in his amusement.

Grimly, I drove back to the Holiday Inn and, leaving the still near-apoplectic Laker to recount the tale to the members of the television team who had preceded us, I telephoned the central police station. The constable at the other end was sympathetic and when I mentioned that my front seat passenger had been one J. C. Laker the officer's voice immediately took on a note of concern. 'Is Mr Laker all right?' he asked anxiously. 'Are you sure? He's just back on the commentary today, isn't he?' When I reported this to the object of the constable's solicitude, over dinner, he choked again. Clearly my motoring misfortunes had a distinctly therapeutic effect.

Jim got to the ground before me the following day. To the wall of the radio commentary box, next door to television's, I found pinned an advertisement cordially inviting me to dine at a certain Chinese restaurant. From my other colleagues, there was merely a large measure of mock sympathy.

Naturally enough, as an international cricketer who had become a television personality, Jim had considerable appeal as an after-dinner speaker and it was good to see that he did not go over the top in asking astronomical fees for his services. This in an era where some of the most insignificant characters have only to appear once on the nation's small screens to put a four-figure sum on their entertainment value. Jim kept things very much within reason and often helped beneficiaries and other very much more charitable causes by appearing for nothing. He was not as polished a speaker as, say, J. J. Warr; but as with his broadcasting, he declined to play a part and concentrated instead on relating a selection of his fund of anecdotes in the homespun way which came naturally to him. He had, of course, a considerable repertoire of stories and I think the one he enjoyed telling best of all was of touring with a Commonwealth XI in up-country India and playing in one of the formerly princely states. It was, he recalled, the only ground where he saw the heavy roller being pulled by an elephant. George Tribe, that brilliant, left-arm purveyor of 'funny stuff' (wrong-'uns) who played for Northamptonshire for most of the 1950s, was having trouble impressing a local umpire with the validity of his appeals for lbw.

Six times in one over George asked and was refused. When the same thing happened off the first ball of his next over he had had enough. Grabbing the umpire by the scruff of the neck, Tribe literally shook him and demanded, 'Have another look you silly ass!' (or words to that effect). The startled umpire wriggled free, gazed earnestly down the pitch and delivered a more acceptable verdict: 'By Jove you are right, Mr Tribe. Batsman, you are out.'

An occasion, however, which revealed its funny side rather later was when in 1981, after a successful London debut at the Barbican, Brian Johnston took his stage show on tour in the provinces. This was the most wholesome and delightful of winter entertainments for cricket-lovers – a couple of films of great cricket from the past, one more up-to-date screening, and then cricket chat involving Brian and three other guests, one of whom was usually Jim Laker. They filled the Colston Hall, Bristol, and a little later, the Theatre Royal, York, where Brian had arranged as his guests, J. C. Laker, F. S. Trueman and myself. Fred was late in arriving (for a change!) and when he finally put in an appearance, Brian was already on stage doing a 'warm-up' to keep the audience from becoming too restive at the delay while Jim and I had a quiet drink in the Green Room. Suddenly, Fred roared in with all guns blazing. He was currently having a bad time in the middle of the controversy which at that time had torn Yorkshire cricket apart. Geoffrey Boycott regarded F. S. T. as his most implacable foe and as he had as his firm allies the cricket writers of the *Yorkshire Post* and *Yorkshire Evening Post* he was able to direct a substantial literary barrage in the direction of the county's greatest fast bowler. When Jim Laker joined the debate with a reasonably mild but definitely Boycott-orientated offering in the *Daily Express*, Fred regarded this as the last straw. He had not realised until rather late in the day that he was to share a platform with Jim at York – the first time they had seen each other since the *Daily Express* article appeared – and he pondered for a long time whether to turn up or not. When he did, it was first to launch a violent verbal assault upon J. C. who tried vainly to turn away his wrath with a soft answer. Fred was not to be appeased and as I stepped (literally) between them I had a quick glimpse from the wings of Brian Johnston's anguished expression as he stood, centre stage, trying to keep the audience happy while his three guests could be seen, out of the corner of his eye, very nearly locked in physical combat at stage left. We managed to get through the evening without any public manifestation of private rancour but Fred stormed off home immediately after the showing – thus missing an extremely pleasant party.

There were many big names, big personalities and big egos around when Laker joined the BBC television commentary team but he slipped easily into the idiom just as on his first appearance before the cameras at Cambridge in that Cavaliers match he had taken to it, in producer Alan Mouncer's words, like a duck to water. Nick Hunter, now Assistant

Head of Sport in BBC television, feels that, 'he and Richie developed into one of the strongest partnerships sport has had on television and his canny professional approach which he had when he was playing was very much his commentary style'. Peter West, for so long the anchorman of TV cricket coverage, had much the same view. Writing before Jim's death, he referred to their 'total unflappability even in the hairiest of crises' and felt that Jim's wry, laconic sense of humour and an anecdote about almost every game in which he played ought to lighten the winter of a cricket's discontent with hours of reminiscence on the box. (If television never got round to doing this, radio did because in 1977 I put together a series of programmes for Radio 4 on the humour of sport and with a panel of J. C. Laker, Peter Parfitt and Neil Hawke, the Australian fast bowler who lived for some years in Lancashire after retirement from first-class cricket, we recorded half-an-hour of merry quip and jest at Oakbank Grammar School, in Keighley, Yorkshire.)

Peter Walker, after four seasons competing with Laker in County Championship cricket, joined him in television coverage of Sunday cricket in the 1970s and very quickly got his first taste of that sardonic humour which could make its point with laserlike penetration. 'Not long after taking over from Frank Bough as the anchorman on BBC 2 cricket presentation', Walker recalls,

> I was eager to stamp my own personality on the job and opened up the programme with a detailed look at both teams and where I felt their strengths and weaknesses lay. At the end of this monologue I handed over to Jim. He began with, 'Thank you, Peter. There's not much left to say,' and left a long meaningful silence to rub home the point! I never again attempted to hog the limelight when working with Jim.

Personally, I regard that as showing a touch of cruelty in the Laker personality but there was a precedent for it which was probably not unknown to Jim. John Arlott – like most of us – resented radio presenters cue-ing over to correspondents for one-minute reports with long, rambling links which covered most of the salient factors of the day up to that point. He listened to one such monologue one Saturday, paused for just long enough to cause concern in the studio – had they lost the line to the commentary point? – and then drawled, with acid emphasis, 'You've said it all. Back to the studio.'

Walker took the hint, and without resentment as others might have done (broadcasters being, in some cases, touchy people) and subsequently always played second fiddle to Jim. He knew better than most that behind Laker's occasionally curt and dismissive manner was concealed an amusing and entertaining companion and Peter worked on the same basis as all who knew Jim reasonably well: he had to like you before he would even share the confidence of his humour. In other words, if he took the mickey it was evidence of a basic regard or affection of some kind; this in turn meant that his friends had to exhibit a certain degree of masochism! He delighted in making life difficult for Bob Duncan, at one time producer of the Sunday League cricket on BBC 2, who knew a good deal about production but not too much about the game and even less about the mysteries of the fixture list. In the run-up to the end of the season with two or three possible winners vying for the championship, Duncan tried to plan ahead by wrestling with the fixtures which remained. For as long as he could sustain the position, Jim remained obdurately unhelpful: 'Essex v Northants? – no chance. It will have no bearing on the championship by the time we get to that game ... Somerset and Derbyshire – I can't get there. I've a dinner in the north of Scotland on the night before the match.' He drove Duncan into a frenzy of despair, right up to the point where the producer was seriously contemplating early retirement, before he relented.

Peter Walker provides us with a rare glimpse of a Laker compliment, too. After one of Peter's tea-time interviews with a player, Jim might saunter across and remark, 'Enjoyed that', and it said more than 1,000 more effusive words. In fact to Walker 'those two words remain as satisfying a memory as that hundred I scored against Jim and the rest of the England attack at Swansea those 30 long years ago'. (Glamorgan v Surrey – his maiden first-class century.)

Wendy Wimbush, the television scorer (a young lady who has discovered the statistician's ideal: scorer at Tests in England in the summer and in Australia during our winter) confesses to having been 'terrified' of Jim in the early stages of her career, even though she afterwards became a family friend with a great affection for Jim and Lilly. Her earlier fears no doubt sprang, in part, from an occasion when a trendy young man from *The Times* – all hair and beard – arrived at a Test to interview Wendy. (Or 'Wimbers' as she even calls herself, inevitably after some time in proximity to Brian Johnston!)

Jim, modest in so many ways, was not without a certain egotism in others, and he watched in some surprise as the interview proceeded. He was there; Richie Benaud and Ted Dexter and company were around. Why then, was Mr Simon Barnes interviewing Wendy Wimbush? Finally he simply had to ask Wimbers, in genuine puzzlement (at the same time getting in a social comment on the appearance of the interviewer!): 'What did Jesus Christ want to talk to *you* about?'

But back to Peter Walker for a most revealing comment on the real Jim Laker: 'To look on as Jim played on the boundary edge with Jamie, his first grandson, was to see a Laker of warmth, love and compassion which few close to him in other ways would have believed possible.'

There was one occasion in 1971 when Jim talked probably more in a commentary than he was ever to do in the future. It had nothing to do with his relative inexperience at that time and I can't think of anyone who blamed him, because a pretty large percentage of the population of this country were caught up in the excitement. This was the Lancashire v Gloucestershire Gillette Cup game which finished at six minutes to nine in the evening and at a time when the BBC's mid-evening news was transmitted at 8.50 p.m., Jim went 'live' into the bulletin to describe one of the most fantastic finishes ever seen. Brian Johnston and I were operating next door for radio so the game will always remain fresh in our own minds. There were so many different facets of the match which have gone into the folklore of the game.

Arthur Jepson was the senior umpire and his colleague was the 38-year-old Dickie Bird in only his second season on the first-class list. There had been some stoppage during the match but if, in the opinion of the umpires, the game could be finished in one day, play could continue after 7.30. Without any way of knowing just how things would turn out, the umpires decreed that a finish could be achieved so, before a full house the game went on and on and on ... Now those at home who watched on television could have no possible idea of just how dark the evening became; the artificial illumination of their screens gave a completely misleading impression and when Dickie, these days, offers the light to batsmen in what seems to spectators to be bright sunshine, I often find myself wondering how much he is influenced by that game so early in his umpiring career. Many times since then he has confessed, 'I was frightened to death that somebody was going to get killed. There was Prockie [Mike Procter] thundering in past me and I could hardly see t'batsman at t'other end. I don't know what I would have done if there had been an appeal for lbw. But he was bowling like a demon an' it were damn near pitch black.'

At the other end, however, was John Mortimore, bowling off-spin to David Hughes who, 16 years later, was to become Lancashire's captain, and in one dramatic over starting at a quarter to nine, Hughes hit him for 4–6–2–2–4–6 to score 24 from six deliveries. Suddenly and improbably, victory was within Lancashire's grasp, and it was then that Dickie Bird had to endure an over of Procter thunderbolts from his end to Lancashire's captain at that time, Jackie Bond.

As the crowd, apparently never quite sure whether the game was won or lost, continually delayed things still further by frequent invasions of the pitch, Jim in the television commentary box, simply could not stop talking. Maybe he felt that viewers found it just as difficult as those of us in the ground did to see what was happening; or if he was merely caught up in the intense excitement of the occasion (which is more likely) he was in exactly the same state of mind as everyone else. As he described, with complete accuracy, the placement of every shot in the over in which Hughes took 24 off Mortimore, he was in just as much of a frenzy as the rest of us ... 'Now we are getting the football crowd ... the chantin' and the singin' ... the lights are on in the pavilion, lights in the dressing-room, lights everywhere ...' Then came Procter's over which was to be the last of the match. Dickie Bird stroked his hands nervously through his hair – five balls with no run scored and after each there was a minor invasion of the pitch and finally Bond negotiated (one can put it no higher than that) the last one out on the off-side and he and Hughes scampered a single. It took Lancashire through to a final which they won and as Brian Johnston and I left the ground some time later we ran into Jim making his way out. We looked at each other and no words were needed; we just rolled our eyes and went on our several ways.

It was a game which brought one of the great remarks in the history of the game – and just how many, one might ask, have been attributable to umpires? When Bond joined Hughes at the crease he looked hard at umpire Jepson and asked, 'What about it, then?' 'What about what?' replied Jepson defiantly (conscious that the game had got into a situation he certainly hadn't envisaged when decreeing that a finish could be achieved). 'The light,' said Bond. 'That's what about it.' Jepson looked contemplatively up into the sky, pointed to the bright silver ball floating across the heavens. 'What's that?' he demanded. 'It's th'moon,' snarled the Lancashire captain. 'That's what I'm talking about. That's th'moon up there.' 'Well,' retorted Jepson, 'that's 260,000 miles away. How far d'you want to see?' And the game proceeded. How I wish we had known of that exchange at the time.

THE
PACKER AFFAIR

We have touched on several aspects of the Laker-Benaud relationship but there are other, equally interesting manifestations to explore, particularly if we move back to 1958 when they were on opposite sides as players in Australia and when Richie was the opposition captain. Shortly after the tour Jim wrote that,

> Benaud fell from grace a little in his behaviour when wickets fell. Almost in the manner of a professional soccer player he would rush around, all but embracing those concerned. I'm all for enthusiasm in its proper place but I felt this behaviour did little for the dignity of the game of cricket.

It is, perhaps, a little difficult to a later generation, accustomed to Benaud's superbly laid-back commentary technique, to picture him rushing around his players in that way but as a young cricketer he certainly brought an enthusiasm, refreshing in some ways, to the game. His comment on that period today, looking back 30 years is,

> I don't know that Jim was unimpressed by my enthusiasm when we *first* met, in 1953 – I think his reaction applied more to the moment when I became captain and I came in for some criticism from Australian commentators like Jack Fingleton and one or two others, which I attempted to counter with an explanation of why I was enthusiastic. Australia in my time had never won a series against England and I had just been thrust into the captaincy. If I wanted to be enthusiastic, then I would be enthusiastic. If it didn't suit everyone then I'd probably have to tone it down; I didn't find any reason to do so in my first year. I think I probably toned it down a little later on but I always remained enthusiastic about cricket and in particular I remained enthusiastic about winning.
>
> Fingleton, in fact, came to see me in Sydney at the end of the series against England in 1958–59 and asked specifically about the fact that I had been more demonstrative on the field than previous captains – Craig, Johnson, Hassett, Bradman and Woodfull. I didn't consider whether I was more demonstrative or not; my reaction was that I was simply *different*. I wanted, if possible, to bustle England out of the game ... out of their established pattern. It was a policy of 'hem them in and bustle them out'. Hence Fingleton, in his book *Four Chukkas*,

talks about a policy of 'hem and bustle'.

It was indeed our policy as established at the first team meeting before the Test in Brisbane. It was also to be part of the policy of coping with Laker and Lock. Coincidentally, it led to one incident which, I think, provides a good insight into the Laker sense of humour. I had been hemming and bustling for all I was worth on the opening day at the Gabba when we bowled England out for 134 on what was a very green pitch. Now a major point of our tactics in the series was to do everything we could to prevent England's bowlers from damaging the wicket in their follow-through because of what had happened a fortnight earlier during the match between an Australian XI and MCC in Sydney. Fred Trueman had created footmarks which provided a target for Lock, and he was then unplayable. Whenever he hit the Trueman footmarks the ball kicked to hit batsmen in the back and about the body. So we didn't want any more of that. There was no specific law at that time to prohibit a bowler from following through onto the 'business' part of the pitch, so we had to devise our own response. From the very first ball bowled, Jimmy Burke studiously and rather ostentatiously patted down the area of the bowler's foot-mark, just to let the umpire know we were keeping an eye on that aspect of things. Somehow Jim Laker had learned of our policy, even before we had had a chance to draw attention to the bowlers' follow-through. He was batting towards the end of the England innings and I was busy setting a field when I noticed, out of the corner of my eye, Jim slowly and quite deliberately walking down the *centre* of the pitch, middle stump to middle stump! I was just starting to erupt with something like, 'Excuse me, James, but would you mind terribly getting off our bloody pitch,' when something stopped me – a small smile playing around his lips.

Instinctively, I looked down and then realised that he was wearing crepes, not spikes. As I quickly discarded the idea of saying anything, the little smile developed just a fraction more. Jim had made his point.

That first divergence of views related to a time when probably neither of them – certainly it was true in Jim's case – visualised an era when they would work in harness as a broadcasting team of the highest quality. The next major occasion on which they found themselves on different sides, however, came when they were operating together as commentators. This was in 1977–78 when Kerry Packer divided the entire cricketing world by setting up his World Series in Australia after signing up many – perhaps one might even say most – of the leading players in the world to play for him. This was not a straightforward case of the two friends having quite different views on Packer's revolutionary concept; not by any means.

When Packer first sprang his new series upon a startled cricket world (piqued by the refusal of the Australian Board of Control to grant him exclusive rights to televise cricket on the commercial Channel 9 which he owned), Laker had in fact a good deal of sympathy with the newspaper and television magnate's point of view. For some years Jim had heard the restive murmurings throughout the game about poor rates of pay, the difficulty in establishing a sound future after playing days were over and often primitive conditions of employment. There can be little doubt that by 1977, in this country at any rate, county cricketers' wages had not kept pace with the huge forward leaps in the cost of living. The time and conditions were undoubtedly right for some form of revolution. What Jim objected to, along with a considerable body of opinion in England, was the 'sneaky' way in which he felt Tony Greig – at that time England's captain! – had played a major role as Packer's agent in this country. After wintering in Australia in 1975–76 (when England had no tour), Greig let it be known that he intended returning to Sydney the following winter (when England did have a tour to India) and it soon became pretty obvious that the charismatic and successful England captain felt that his future lay in Australia. This led to a forthright article by Jim in the *Daily Express*, questioning Greig's application to the role of England captain and making it clear that he (Laker) felt Greig's first priority should concern English cricket. Greig immediately asked the *Express* for a right of reply. When this courtesy was accorded him he wrote an article in which he said it was an honour to be England's captain and if selected he would be willing to tour India the following winter. He did, in fact, lead England on the sub-continent, and successfully, too, as England won the series by three Tests to one with the final match drawn. That tour ended in February, 1977; by May the story had broken of the World Series matches to be staged in Australia during 1978–79 with most of the best players in the West Indies and Australia contracted to take part in them along with a number from England, India, Pakistan and South Africa at salaries ranging from $40,000 (Australian) down to $16,500. Packer was in England himself during the summer of 1977 and quietly did a bit of recruiting of his own to add to his television commentary team for his series. It then emerged that Richie Benaud's public relations firm, based in Sydney, was prominently involved in setting up the Series.

Richie at that time (and since that time, as well) kept a low profile about the extent of his involvement, but clearly he had discussions with Jim which neither man has ever disclosed in any detail. What Jim has said about a time which caused the most serious upheaval in the whole history of the game is this:

I have the greatest admiration for Richie. He was a magnificent cricketer – in my view the best captain Australia have produced in my time and that included Sir Donald Bradman. As a cricket commentator he is far ahead of anyone I have heard in any part of the world and never have I met a more industrious, hard-working yet generous ex-cricketer in my career. The [Packer] contracts offered to the players were made public but there has never been a figure published for the Benaud contract. It must surely have been out of this world and not for one minute would I criticise Richie for accepting it. Benaud's cricketing advice to Packer was to prove invaluable, particularly in respect of players who were offered contracts and his insistence that WSC had to be played as strictly as possible to the laws of the established game. Here he met some resistance from several of the non-cricketing executives who would have been happier to overrule some of the finer and acknowledged points of the game in favour of the razzmatazz of a wandering road show. Happily, on most counts, Benaud had his way.

Of course, in accepting the appointment, Richie lost many friends. He was blackballed by the Australian Board of Control and his great friend (and room-mate for much of his playing career) Neil Harvey just about disowned him. He also received pretty short shrift from Sir Donald Bradman. For years he had been welcomed by one and all in England, yet while he still retained the friendship of a good percentage of Englishmen (myself included) there remained a good many who cut him dead. Indeed, the unhappiest feature in cricket since Kerry Packer appeared on the scene is the sudden ending of life-long friendships which since the game was first played have been a pleasant feature of cricketers' lives.

That was Jim's view in 1979. A decade later he might well have added that a residual effect was the changing of players' attitudes to the game in a way in which pride in playing for one's country was pushed to a large extent into the background. I am sure that grim smile would have appeared as the smoke cleared and Australia emerged as the country most adversely affected in the aftermath of the World Series. But it would have been a smile which reflected no pleasure.

Jim was invited by Packer, personally, to join his commentary team, which was headed by Richie and was to include a number of former Australian Test players with little or no experience of broadcasting, and the experienced Tony Cozier as a West Indian voice to accompany the television pictures. The verbal invitation was followed a few days later by a lucrative contract sent to his agent which would have given him just about the same income for eight weeks in the Australian summer as he gained from three years working for the BBC. In less than 24 hours Jim had turned down the offer and Fred Trueman went to provide an English voice on the Channel 9 commentary team.

In January, 1979, I met Jim in Sydney where we had both watched a certain amount of World Series cricket being played and viewed with interest the televising of the matches. He reported that if he had harboured any doubts about the wisdom of turning down Packer's offer they had very quickly been dispersed after listening to the 'biased, loaded, non-critical commentary'. My own reaction was similar which makes it particularly interesting to read Richie Benaud's reflections, elsewhere in this book, on his respect for David Hill, the Channel 9 cricket producer. It may be that the style has changed from that artificially hyped, nonstop babble of platitudinous claptrap which went on in 1978–79 to describe the World Series but, after listening to Channel 9's commentary during the last three Australian summers (the commercial channel having wrested commentary on official Test cricket from the Australian Broadcasting Corporation) it is difficult to say that it has changed to a very great extent. True, we no longer have a frenetic compulsion on the part of the commentators to build up the World Series into a credible rival to orthodox Test cricket, but Australian viewers are still subjected to non-stop prattling, often of the most infantile kind, from former players who have never taken the trouble to learn lessons from David Hill, from Richie Benaud, or from anyone else. Viewers still have to suffer the indignity of that cartoon duck waddling across the screen when a batsman fails to trouble the scorer; they still have to endure advertisements intruding where a few words of enlightenment from an expert comments-man would be appropriate. Perhaps the Australians like it!

Technically, the Channel 9 coverage of World Series cricket was of a very high standard, with money apparently no object in the number of cameras employed and modern play-back technology used to review every shot and every delivery from every conceivable angle. But there became a very serious danger of overkill and what the two of us found most unfortunate was the way the great accumulation of hardware was used to expose flaws in the decisions of umpires. The Packer era has left behind a number of unfortunate legacies to international cricket and this is undoubtedly one of the worst, as it lingers on in almost every country in the world. Another was the placing of microphones near the stumps, ostensibly to provide a more dramatic range of sound effects but here again, in the winter of 1987–88 in particular, we have seen side-effects which have been seriously damaging to the image of the game.

Packer's circus had a devastating effect upon Test cricket on a wide scale. It led to a High Court action in England which Packer won hands down. It produced turmoil in a number of county clubs where players had signed contracts to play for Packer, notably Kent (Knott, Underwood, Woolmer, Asif Iqbal, Bernard Julien), Warwickshire (Dennis Amiss), Sussex (Greig – of course – and John Snow) and even Nottinghamshire, where Clive Rice had just been appointed captain and had the office taken away from him. And Packer, it has to be said, scored a huge populist victory when plans for his new project were given an airing on British television screens. Laker had publicly stated his case: while sympathetic in many ways to Packer's ideas and approving of the fact that they might well loosen a rather feudalistic grip on professional cricketers' lives and earnings, he could not stomach 'the underhand way in which establishment cricket had been stabbed in the back'. He agreed at once, therefore, when asked to represent the traditional standpoint on David Frost's television programme which at that time enjoyed very high viewing-figures. Many people might have felt daunted at the prospect – Frost was adept at framing the most searching questions and did not easily allow anyone to escape with anything less than full and frank answers. Kerry Packer himself was to be a part of the programme and he was known to be an extremely tough and uncompromising opponent. It was going to be a particularly difficult assignment.

I remember discussing these very points with Jim shortly before the programme and I was mildly surprised at the complete *sang froid* with which he approached the occasion. More than that; he was actually looking forward to it. Quite simply he believed he had some sound and valid arguments to put forward; he felt orthodox cricket had a good case and that he could plead it with honesty and clarity. Feeling no personal animosity to Packer he saw no reason to doubt that the Frost programme would yield a series of intelligent, reasoned and illuminating arguments on both sides. All these hopes were dashed when Robin Marlar entered the lists as a fourth contributor to the evening. A Cambridge Blue and former Sussex captain, Marlar became a pungent and often controversial cricket writer with *The Sunday Times*. He had, in fact, been a friend of Jim's since his university days when Laker did some coaching at Fenner's but his arrival on the scene did not inspire Jim with confidence about the way the television debate might go. Marlar held strong, and often peculiar views on a number of subjects and was well known as a man who would stand his ground as a minority of one against the rest of the world just as easily — perhaps even more comfortably — than as a member of a large majority. It is possible that his close connection with the Sussex club, which felt a keen sense of betrayal at Tony Greig's hands, influenced the way he now sailed into battle with Packer with a religious zeal which bordered on the fanatical. Laker, hoping to be heard as the voice of sweet reason and commonsense, was scarcely able to get into the argument; Frost, watching with sardonic amusement, found his probes largely superfluous. Marlar argued with passionate emotion; Packer replied with icy logic. He held Marlar at verbal arm's length, toying with him. As Jim saw it, 'Robin completely lost his self-control and was quietly and clinically taken apart by Packer.'

The studio audience, as I saw the programme, was hardly a cross-section of the cricketing public looking for enlightenment on two points of view. All too clearly the members were top-heavy with those who saw this as an issue between the fuddy-duddies of the cricketing establishment as represented by Lord's and an invigorating broom of new thinking wielded by the antipodean reformer, and those in the audience who might have started out with an open mind were quickly alienated by Marlar's irrational performance. The debate ended with Packer a clear winner — by an innings, as Jim put it.

At the end of the debate, however, Jim was keenly interested to have a long talk with Packer about his plans for cricket coverage. As a commentator he was particularly intrigued by the plans to have eight cameras recording events — twice the number normally used by the BBC at that time — and it was during this chat that the tycoon made his first approach to Jim to work for Channel 9. It cost him a good deal of money to turn down the offer, as we have seen, just as it did with several leading English players and the umpire, Dickie Bird. One likes to think that none of them has regretted the decision. Packer's influence on world cricket was profound and far from generally beneficial. Having watched something of the 1979 World Series in operation I crossed the Tasman Sea to commentate on the New Zealand v Pakistan series and was appalled by the attitude of some of the tourists, coming fresh from the Channel 9 circus. The age of bad manners had arrived in international cricket.

THE
'SPIN TWINS'

It has been a matter of journalistic convenience, especially to those who write headlines, to refer to slow bowlers who operate in tandem over the years as 'spin twins'. With the possible exception of the West Indies pair, Ramadhin and Valentine, the pair who have been most frequently bracketed together would have to be Jim Laker and Tony Lock. Yet while 'twins' implies a closeness, physical similarities and a certain unanimity of tastes and interests, a more dissimilar pair than the Surrey 'twins' would be difficult to find. Laker was every inch a townie from the industrial north; Lock a country boy from picturesque rural Surrey, born in Limpsfield and arriving at The Oval via Oxted Cricket Club.

Jim was fatherless from the age of two; Tony's development as a cricketer was lovingly superintended by a devoted father. The dour, undemonstrative northerner was a mature 25-year-old with five years of wartime service behind him when they first met; the volatile and voluble southerner was a raw 17 and a half. They rarely spent any of their spare moments together as Surrey players and when they joined forces for England, Lock tended to seek the companionship of a kindred spirit like Freddie Trueman while Jim was happier spending his evenings talking cricket over a beer with the quieter and more thoughtful members of the tour party. But put them together on the field and it was a different story altogether. Their aggregate of first-class victims was 4,788 and it is unlikely that there has ever been a combination in which the bowling partners complemented each other to anything like the same extent. Both were tremendous spinners of the ball and used turn (or on occasions, the threat of turn) more than flight. Laker instanced Denis Compton and Doug Insole (Essex) as good players of off-spin bowling whom he would have expected to score more heavily against him with a less threatening partner than Lock at the other end. On the other hand, Len Hutton and Don Kenyon (of Worcestershire) were adept at dealing with the slow left-armer but much less at home against his off-spinning colleague. Lock, who lost much of his thatch of thick red hair at a relatively early age, fielded in Jim's leg-trap on a turning pitch at Bristol very early in their partnership and dropped four catches in the first hour. It brought a comment from Jim to the captain which he recalled with a wry smile throughout the remainder of his career: 'Do the kid a favour and stick him on the boundary. He'll never be a short-leg as long as he plays the game.'

It was a put-down which Lock, too, was to resurrect many times with great glee as the line 'c Lock, b Laker' began to appear with greater frequency than any other in county scorecards.

Originally, Lock used flight to a far greater extent than he was to do in the greater part of his bowling career and at that time his lack of spin was noticeable when the two of them were operating together on rain-affected pitches. At the end of the 1950 season, therefore, we see the first close co-operation of the two men who had hitherto been fairly distant colleagues. Together they discussed, and experimented with, a new Lock style of bowling – a little quicker and increasing the degree of spin. Jim went off to New Zealand after that, leaving Tony to practice through the winter in an indoor school in Croydon. And here something happened which was to have a considerable effect upon Lock's bowling future: the nets at Allder's School were not high enough to allow anything like a spin bowler's trajectory when Lock, a tallish young man, delivered the ball with a fully-extended arm. The tragedy was that there seems to have been no one around to spot what was happening and to put him right. The result was that he spent the whole of the winter bowling with a very long delivery-stride and a slightly bent left arm delivering the ball at a lower height. He returned to the Surrey nets for the start of the 1951 season with his entire bowling style changed, from the rhythm of his approach to a suspiciously jerky delivery when he bowled a quicker ball. Jack Parker, the veteran all-rounder, looked across at Jim and breathed, 'He'll never get away with it.' And it did not take long for the word to go round the county circuit: 'Lockie is chucking it.' He now imparted tremendous spin and Laker quickly found himself being left behind in the pair's annual chase to be first to 100 wickets. It was all, in Gilbertian terms, 'calculated to cause remark', and so it did. In a match against Essex, Doug Insole regarded a flattened middle-stump and inquired of anyone who might be listening, 'Was I bowled, or run-out?' When Keith Miller, touring with the 1953 Australians, heard the ball thwack into Arthur McIntyre's wicketkeeping gloves as he was half way through his pick-up he sardonically commented, 'Strike one'. And on the 1953–54 MCC tour to West Indies the legendary George Headley was left with only one stump standing after Lock had bowled a quicker one and he left the field with a heartfelt, 'Dis ain't cricket, man. Dis is war.'

In Jamaica, on that tour, Lock was actually 'called' for throwing in a First Test which was stormy enough in other ways. Lock was also no-balled in the second innings and with murmurings on the home circuit becoming more restive he finally reverted to his old style – and was still a magnificent bowler! His last season for Surrey, however, was in 1963 and he then alternated between Western Australia (1962–63 to 1970–

71) and Leicestershire (1965–67) where his role as an experienced spinner played a major part in creating a more successful side than the county had previously known.

In the days when Lock was regarded with the gravest suspicion in English, and international, cricketing circles Laker refused to join those who felt his partner was an out-and-out 'chucker', while accepting that his quicker ball (and it was quick) was delivered with an extremely suspect action. While they were never close as team-mates, there was a profound mutual respect born of intense rivalry. No doubt the huge differences in temperament and personality emphasised that intensity. Jim might have had a few reservations about certain aspects of his colleague's action, but if anyone outside the Surrey circle offered a critical view he was quick and thunderous in his defence.

The rivalry between Lock and Johnny Wardle for the slow left-armer's place in the England side was fierce and bitter in an entirely different way. Wardle, a superb bowler, had the Yorkshire player's deep-seated belief that if you played for Surrey you were automatically looked upon more favourably than anyone from the northern counties in general and the white rose county in particular. He was, along with most of his team-mates, strongly of the view that Lock got many wickets with illegal deliveries which went unnoticed by umpires. Jim Laker, while appreciating Wardle's talent as a cricketer did not like him as a man and therefore it seemed to me at times when we discussed the two of them, that his pro-Lock sentiments owed a little more to team loyalty than dispassionate assessment. In some ways I am sure he rather enjoyed the occasion of a confrontation between the two left-armers on the occasion of Wardle's Benefit match at Bradford in 1957. Lock was bowling when the Beneficiary came to the wicket expecting – as tradition entitled him to do – to be given 'one off the mark'.

Almost pleadingly, Lock asked his skipper (P. B. H. May in his first season as the Surrey leader), 'I don't really have to give *him* one, do I, skipper?' The captain politely insisted that the niceties must be observed and so Wardle received a gentle one, outside the off-stump, which he pushed for the single. But Wardle, too, was a man who liked to make a point. He once told me, 'I knew damn well it would break Lockie's heart to give me a run so I thought I'd make him sweat a bit.' He did – by taking the single very quickly indeed and giving the impression that he was going to try to make it into two. Lock was certainly not going to carry generosity to that extent and hared after the ball himself, swooped and spun round with arm raised, ready to hurl it to the wicketkeeper.

He then saw Wardle leaning on his bat at the non-striker's end, shaking with laughter. Point to Wardle.

It was ironic that Lock accompanied Laker to Australia for the only time in 1958–59 because Wardle (who had been chosen) had his invitation to tour withdrawn as a result of his *Daily Mail* articles following his Yorkshire dispute with the 1958 captain, Ronnie Burnet – a dispute which ended his first-class career. It was not a successful tour for Lock, for whose style the pitches were not entirely suitable and in some ways it was also a sad one. As the tour party moved on to New Zealand he saw a film of his bowling action and at last accepted that at some stages of his delivery it was open to the suspicions which he had heard, and shrugged off, during the previous seven or eight years. He set out to reconstruct the action, not suddenly and dramatically, but over a period of time and he was, in fact, able to bowl through the last years of his career without complaint. In 1962–63 he spent the winter enjoying an Australian summer and playing for Western Australia and he decided that his and his family's future lay out there. He completed his contract with Surrey in 1963, then emigrated to Australia where he played a leading part in the development of Western Australia into a major power in Sheffield Shield cricket and the inclusion of the Waca Ground on the list of Test Match venues. Amongst those who followed him to Western Australia were Peter Loader and Ron Tindall, former Surrey team-mates, but he was not entirely lost to English cricket. Indeed, far from it.

In 1965, Mike Turner – the enterprising and imaginative secretary-manager of Leicestershire – persuaded Tony to sign a three-year contract and in 1966 he took over the captaincy. Leicestershire, conditioned by years of modest performance in county cricket and with no great tradition of junior cricket to provide new blood, found in G. A. R. Lock exactly the sort of dynamic and competitive leadership which had been missing for so long. In 1966, Leicestershire achieved eighth position in the county championship table with their captain taking 109 wickets with a blameless action and in 1967 they were runners-up to Yorkshire (Lock, 128 wickets at 18.11 apiece).

How was this achieved? Let Laker tell us about that:

His enthusiasm was infectious and he led by example in every depart-
ment of the game. He imbued the side with the belief that they were
as good as any other and taught them never to give up hope. It is
quite astonishing that in a short space of time he had worked the
oracle with two sides 10,000 miles apart. A further season with

Leicestershire became out of the question when he was suddenly beset by a number of domestic problems which demanded his staying in Perth. Yet even now he was not finally finished with English cricket. In a dramatic dash to the West Indies to reinfore Colin Cowdrey's 1967–68 touring side (because of an accident to Fred Titmus) he played in the last two Tests and at Georgetown, Guyana, shared a record ninth-wicket partnership of 109 with Pat Pocock (of Surrey!) to save the series. If I know my Tony, the 89 he made in Georgetown gave him more satisfaction than any bowling performance in any Test.

So much for Laker on Lock – now what about Lock on Laker? First, short-leg fielding:

Fielding at short-leg to Jim Laker is a joy (this in 1957). He is a text-book off-spinner in technique and temperament and maintains such a beautiful length that one is consistently expecting a catch in the leg-trap – that is when the ball is biting. When I take up my position my attitude can be summed up like this: I think my fielding helps Jim's bowling and I *know* his bowling helps my fielding. I stand as close as possible to snap up those catches which merely lob off the bat but not so close that I miss the fast snicks. The position, of course, depends on the pace of the pitch and the extent to which the ball is turning.

Nearly 40 years on there is still an air of bewilderment as Lock talks of Laker's attitude as a bowler:

He never said whether he was pleased or sorry about his bowling. The odd slight grin, or shrug of the shoulders, would be the only indication that he had any opinion at all about what had happened. I was completely different. My appeals were louder. I *demanded* the umpire give batsmen out and I swore when he didn't (not at the umpire, of course, but at the injustice of the decision). Jim would take everything in his stride and accept everything as it came – with a calm outlook.

In contrast to Laker's problems with the corn on his main spinning finger, Lock never had to worry about anything of that nature. He did however, have extremely tender skin over the whole of his hands which makes the memory of some of his sizzling catches – off Fred Trueman and Brian Statham, for example, the more remarkable – and when this became, to some extent, public knowledge he was offered a wide-ranging list of possible cures. They ranged from sticking his fingers in a pint of beer (he felt there were other and more important uses for beer), to immersing them in either paraffin or the water in a blacksmith's cooling trough. That latter was probably rather difficult to find in the 1950s; it would be almost impossible today.

Lock's 1957 book has, naturally enough, copious references to Laker but very few of them involve a personal note of any consequence. Checking through the index and then rustling back through the pages one encounters the name of his spinning partner accompanied only by a bowling analysis or sometimes simply the name of another player. There does occur a comment which would seem like heresy to most of their contemporaries — 'Toey Tayfield was the best off-spinner on a plumb wicket I ever saw, Laker the best on a turner —' but anything which indicates a personal warmth is very difficult indeed to discover. Indeed, he was irritated and occasionally downright angry at the different measures adopted by Surridge (and later followed by May) in handling the two spinners: 'While Laker got the kid-glove treatment, I got the needling. This often prompted me into pushing the ball through more quickly and reduced the amount of spin I gave it.'

Opposition batsmen, of course, were not unaware of what was happening and, on occasions, took advantage of it. During the Surrey v Australians game of 1956, as Laker's first all-10 became a distinct possibility, Keith Miller was just the man to take advantage of the situation. While treating Laker with great respect he started to hit Lock back over mid-off — anathema to the slow left-armer whose fury was enhanced when Surridge instructed him, 'For goodness sake, bowl tighter.' Lock reacted predictably and the argument was continued as they both took their places in the leg-trap for Laker's next over from the other end. And it was Miller, inevitably, who extracted the last ounce from the situation. He stepped away from the wicket, looked at the crouching pair to his left and said with only faintly disguised seriousness, 'If you two don't stop needling each other I shall have to report you to the umpire.' Lock was speechless with rage.

Laker and Lock, then, were never close during their long and extremely profitable association on the cricket field. Personal friendship had to wait until 18 years after the professional association had ended. The organisers of the Centenary Test celebrations in Melbourne in 1977 looked merely at their bowling partnership in deciding to pair them together in an hotel room and there, 10,000 miles and nearly two decades later, friendship at last bloomed.

Lock explains:

We were very nearly sharing a bed, let alone a room, because they were only about a foot apart. Anyway, something clicked during the two weeks we were together in Melbourne and at last we became friends. Perhaps I had matured, or Jim had relaxed, but everything ran so smoothly. I felt a genuine and terrible sense of loss when Jim died.

WHAT THE STARS FORETELL

It was while staying at the Laker home in Putney one Saturday evening that I was surprised to find Jim producing, almost sheepishly, a manuscript which he said was being prepared for publication and dealt with matters astrological. The Laker I knew, it seemed to me, would be the first to poo-poo as superstitious nonsense the very idea that stars could govern one's destiny. But Jim – insisting 'it's not as daft as you seem to think; read it', claimed to have discovered some remarkable similarities in style and characteristics amongst cricketers born under the same birth-sign. It was years later that Lilly confessed to having put the idea into Jim's head by pointing out how many points could be found in common amongst Librans, Aquarians and Saggitarians, etc. Jim then browsed through *Wisden* and the first thing he spotted was that the two fine South Africans, Athol Rowan and 'Toey' Tayfield were born, like him, under the sign of the water-carrier. If he was not immediately hooked, he most certainly was when he read that, 'The Aquarian is not in awe of tradition or authority. He will never refrain from turning on those in higher office, particularly when in search for the truth.' Could there possibly be a rebel or two amongst my Aquarian team? he asked himself after producing 11 names – Bill Lawry and Bobby Simpson (Australia), Bev Congdon (New Zealand), Norm O'Neill (Australia), John Hampshire (England), Don Tallon (Australia), Neil Hawke (Australia), Tayfield, Laker, Fred Trueman (England) and Andy Roberts (West Indies). Well, if rebelliousness or simple non-conformism is not especially notable in his batsmen it is most certainly present amongst his bowlers.

Jim was fascinated and his interest grew as he worked on through the birthdays of great players:

Capricorn ('Takes life earnestly and is generally an upholder of tradition and authority') – Peter May, Colin Cowdrey.

Pisces ('Seldom succeeds in making money and rarely accumulates it') – Brian Close, Bill Johnston, prominent followers of the Sport of Kings.

Aries ('Known for their captaincy and leadership') – Bill Edrich, who had a distinguished wartime record as an RAF officer and Ajit Wadekar, 16 times captain of India.

Taurus ('Steadfast in mind, unshaken in adversity and quietly persistent in the face of difficulties') – look no further than opening batsmen Jack Fingleton of Australia and Conrad Hunte of West Indies.

Gemini ('Charming types with many friends, impatient with repetition and with a great desire to express themselves') – Denis Compton and Alan Davidson are superb illustrations.

Cancer ('Can be summed up in one word – patience') – Len Hutton and Sunil Gavaskar certainly fit the bill, but how did Geoff Boycott escape this category?

Leo ('Organisers who understand and appreciate the qualities of other types, consequently making good leaders') – Gary Sobers and Greg Chappell are perhaps better categorised as captains who led by example. One would have thought Mike Brearley fitted in ideally here, but he's a Taurean.

Virgo ('Separates, sifts, classifies and arranges his materials and his men, recognising at a glance the potential value of each and making the best of everyone and everything') – as Jim pointed out at the time, Sir Donald Bradman *had* to be born between 24 August and 23 September), along with Lindsay Hassett and Clive Lloyd.

Libra ('The one who succeeds in life is generally, in one way or another, a specialist') – oh yes indeed. Geoffrey Boycott, Richie Benaud.

Scorpio ('Strong, powerful and muscular with thick-set frame') – no arguments about Ken McKay or Colin McDonald.

Sagittarius ('Universally acclaimed as sportsmen, showing predeliction for outdoor work') – probably the best category of all to illustrate this: Keith Miller, Ian Botham, Trevor Bailey.

As Jim mentioned at the time he was not so much concerned with making a particular point as having an enormous amount of fun from these researches. He produced a good 11 to represent each astrological category and found some really wonderful teams. It is, of course, one of the many aspects of cricket which make such a wonderful game for researchers of every kind. Then he went on to produce a World XI plus a 12th man with one name drawn from each of the 12 categories. This is how it looked: Len Hutton (Cancer), Arthur Morris (Capricorn), Don Bradman (Virgo), captain, Denis Compton (Gemini), Everton Weekes (Pisces), Gary Sobers (Leo), Richie Benaud (Libra), Alan Knott, wk, (Aries), Harold Larwood (Scorpio), Freddie Trueman (Aquarius), Bill O'Reilly (Sagittarius). 12th man: Ted Dexter (Taurus). It certainly looks an unbeatable combination to my eyes. For good measure, Jim added five more names to make up a touring party: Godfrey Evans (Leo), Alec Bedser (Cancer), Vivian Richards (Pisces), Ray Lindwall (Libra) and J. C. Laker, 'with apologies but I am certainly not going to miss out on such a tour'.

Jim's dabbling on the Turf took a more orthodox form. He and Richie Benaud, in fact, enjoyed the contest of finding more winners than each other better than the actual success of a modest flutter. Part of their companionable silence at the start of any commentary day was due to the fact that both of them spent much time studying form – Richie with *Timeform* or *Raceform* notebooks, Jim with the *Sporting Life* and loyally, the *Daily Express*.

Their bets rarely exceeded £1 or 50p. Occasionally Richie might be tempted to go as high as a fiver if he thought he had discovered a particularly good thing. 'I might go three weeks and never have a bet,' says Richie, 'but I would still look at the form every morning because I enjoy it. It's good relaxation. It's the enjoyment of picking a horse you think can win but not necessarily backing it. For me, working out race form is more enjoyable than doing a crossword puzzle (another favourite commentary box and dressing-room occupation). I only half enjoy that, though. Best of all I like going through a whole programme of races, picking a likely winner in each one, then searching the following day's paper to see how I have got on.'

It was a hobby he shared with Jim to a fairly high level of intensity and visitors looking for conversation were not warmly welcomed to the television commentary box in the hour between 10 and 11 a.m. It became a sort of ritual that if you needed to talk to either Jim or Richie about anything you waited until they strolled out of the box. This was an almost regal indication that chat could now begin. Jim strolled more frequently than Richie who can be as sparing with words away from the microphone as he is in front of it. Jim, on the other hand, liked to be kept up to date with happenings in the Bradford League, even 40 years after he played there, and I often had snippets of information for him about which clubs were doing well. But it was infinitely better for him when Ray Illingworth joined the commentary team because he was intimately involved with the Farsley club and, at the time of Jim's death, was actually still playing for Farsley occasionally. Jim's affection for the League was a remarkable thing. He maintained his links with a number of friends, not only at the Saltaire club but in others as well, and it was virtually impossible to persuade him to spend the Sunday of the Headingley Test doing anything but visiting Roberts Park. In that sense he remained every inch a Yorkshireman.

Apart from studying the form book, Jim enjoyed a day at the races with Lilly from time to time but could never persuade her to join in the fun of picking a winner. She would accept his offered fiver or tenner for a bit of a flutter, then put the note in her purse, commenting, 'I'd rather spend it at Sainsbury's.' Loyally, she adds, 'But if I did have a bet and followed Jim's advice, the horse usually won.'

EPILOGUE

James Charles Laker died, after an illness which struck with tragically dramatic suddenness, on 23 April, 1986, in the same 24 hours which also saw the loss to cricket of Bill Edrich. We shall search for a suitable epitaph in a moment but as one nears the end of a book like this, fears arise that something vital may have been missed out and some significant aspect of the Laker story omitted. Rather late in its preparation I received a letter from Peter Iles, who had been a team-mate of Jim's in grade cricket in New Zealand in 1951. Writing 37 years later from California, USA, Mr Iles was anxious that certain matters should not be overlooked:

In New Zealand, Jim volunteered to do much extra work to foster junior cricket. Contacts he made with players while he was with us continued long after that, both at top level amongst men representing New Zealand or playing for English counties, or at lower levels amongst young New Zealanders visiting England.

Throughout his career — as cricketer or broadcaster — Jim always had time to talk to old friends from Yorkshire, or his army days, whenever their paths crossed.

In addition to his many after-dinner speaking engagements of a formal nature, he spent a great deal of time travelling widely (and without payment) to more obscure cricketing backwaters with which an old friend — and sometimes a mere chance acquaintance — might be associated.

At official functions at Lord's or The Oval I have seen him spend more time with relatively unknown guests than with the celebrities on parade from cricket, other sports and the world of entertainment.

Jim had an almost perfect recall for details of his cricketing life and this was not only invaluable as a raconteur but was a key factor in his 'common touch'. But he not only remembered names and faces — he had a genuine interest in the lives of the people he had met. He was not only a good talker; he was a good listener as well.

And then, checking back through a file of research, one happens upon small but significant tributes which have so far slipped through the net, such as John Arlott's:

He gradually and shrewdly worked it out that there was a difference between knowing about cricket and knowing about broadcasting. He became, to my mind, a very good pro on commentary as he had been on cricket. If I stood in awe of him when we first started to work together, I think we ended up even-handed and an extremely friendly pair. I had great affection for him.

Tony Swainson, director of the Lord's Taverners:

He was not an easy man to get close to, but once you had broken down the barrier you were received with open arms. He was, to me, highly intelligent and did not suffer fools gladly.

Mickey Stewart:

He was the best off-spinner I have played with or against or have ever seen. He used to say to me that on any day, on any surface, you could bowl, if you wanted to, a maiden over at any batsman (with the exception, and it was in his earlier days, of Don Bradman). It could be achieved by bowling 'flat'. But that was a term only applied at that time to lesser bowlers because if a slow bowler bowled flat he was thought to lack something.

Peter Walker:

He never forgave the selectors for preferring Jim McConnon in '54–55. He had his disagreements, too, with eminent personages like Peter May but Jim was always an Oval man. In the latter years of his life he used to take great pleasure in telling me of the ambitious development plans he and the members of the Surrey Committee were working on. One of the great tragedies is that he did not live to see them all come to fruition.

And that, indeed, was a period of his life which gave him great satisfaction – the wounds healed, the bitterness put aside, working once again for the greater glory of Surrey. It all came right in the end. And so it is to Surrey that we turn for not one, but two epitaphs, both of which appeared in the Surrey handbook. The first, from Alan de Silva, who lives in Portugal, was in verse:

Old Trafford, Manchester, one summer long ago,
Nigh on twenty years and ten!
You breathed your magic on a ball
And made it float and fizz in flighted fall
From the Stretford End

We had basked in the glory of your deeds
Throughout the weekend rain
Nine wickets in an innings was the best

Against Australia batting in a Test
We would not see its like again.

Or so it seemed that fateful final day
After the luncheon break.
The sun was out, the ball had lost its shine
But the pitch had yet to show some sign
That spin would take.

Four hours left, eight wickets still to take;
Time was your enemy!
And then, in one destructive spell
Four good Australian wickets fell
To you for only three.

Strong nerves were needed to survive
The tension after tea.
Despite Lock's labours at the other end
By innings' close you had all ten
And nineteen for ninety.

No champagne bottles popped above your head,
As we gathered round to cheer.
Modest to the end you raised your hand,
More famous now than any in the land.
It held a glass of beer.

Now you are gone and we will miss the wit
Of your wry commentary.
But the memories of that famous day
Will live with those who saw you make your way
Into cricket history.

Farewell then, Jim Laker, Bradford-born,
Yorkshire bred and Surrey-wed,
A greater spinner England never knew
Around the world they will remember you
Where'er the game is played.

Of course, we now know the truth about that notorious 'glass of beer'!

While it is right to mourn the fact that Jim Laker died while he had still so much to give to the world of cricket – through his broadcasting, his involvement with Surrey, as president of Surrey Schools Cricket and through his friendships which so many people prized so highly – perhaps it is better to remember his life with gratitude for the great cricket he played. From Lilly, after reading this manuscript, came a lovely, loving, backward glance:

> Judging by the 350 letters I had after he died and by the obituary notices in the papers, he was not an unpopular man. He did like to 'stir it up' but there was never any malice in it. He was also a very cautious and careful person and not hasty in making a decision. For instance, he was engaged to be married three times to three different ladies, before me!

The one unfortunate note in the period immediately following Jim's death was, surprisingly, struck by the BBC. Surprisingly because the Corporation is generally a benign and caring employer, certainly to its own staff. Perhaps freelances are not always treated with the same consideration and solicitude. In any event, the BBC, with whom Jim's contract had a long way to run, sent an ex-gratia payment of £100 – which is nowhere near even a day's payment for television commentary. Not for a second does Lilly suggest the amount should have been higher; she would have been very much happier if no payment had been made at all. Less than a day's pay is a rather tasteless acknowledgement of 111 Test Match commentaries and so many other games besides. It was a terrible error of judgement on the part of someone in Television Centre. But let us not end our story on a sour note . . .

It must be right, surely, for the last word to go to Tony Lock. Their friendship took a long time to develop and when it did it was not *in* cricket but *of* cricket. Some might feel it sad that a relationship of personal regard should have lasted less than a decade when their sporting association went back so very much further but it was perhaps pre-ordained that the volatile Lock and the phlegmatic Laker should only become close long after their playing days had ended and they had reached middle-aged maturity. That is how it seems as one reads Lockie's final tribute:

> I have thought a good deal about Jim Laker in the past few months and firmly believe that he is not really dead. It was suddenly decided that his services were required on a much higher level and now he is no doubt discussing tactics with the great players who went before him.

To those of you who saw the great man bowl, you were very lucky, and for those of you less fortunate, you now have to put up with very poor imitations.

CAREER
FIGURES

COMPILED BY
ROBERT BROOKE

Season-by-season record in first-class cricket

	M	I	NO	R	HS	Avge	100	50	Ct	O	M	R	W	Avge	5 WI	10 WM	BB
1946	3	3	1	3	3	1.50	–	–	1	60	12	169	8	21.12	–	–	3/43
1947	18	26	4	408	60	18.54	–	1	13	575.5	135	1420	79	17.97	5	–	8/69
1947–48	8	12	2	212	55	21.20	–	1	4	388.5	117	973	36	27.02	3	–	7/103
1948	29	44	10	828	99	24.35	–	3	16	1058.4	250	2903	104	27.91	4	–	8/55
1949	28	39	7	548	100	17.12	1	–	26	1192.1	419	2422	122	19.85	8	1	8/42
1950	30	42	6	589	53	16.36	–	1	20	1399.5	522	2544	166	15.32	12	5	8/2
1950–51	10	10	1	171	61	19.00	–	1	5	315.2	131	579	36	16.08	3	–	6/23
1951	28	38	6	624	89	19.50	–	4	22	1301.3	400	2681	149	17.99	13	5	7/36
1951–52	4	4	0	77	35	19.25	–	–	3	228.1	88	379	24	15.79	3	1	5/44
1952	30	34	5	310	26	10.68	–	1	15	1070.4	342	2219	125	17.75	9	1	7/57
1953	31	34	3	502	81	16.19	–	1	25	1155.5	382	2366	135	17.52	7	1	6/25
1953–54	7	9	1	123	33	16.62	–	–	4	333.5	113	756	22	34.36	–	–	4/47
1954	29	33	9	607	113	25.29	1	1	29	966.2	315	2048	135	15.17	13	5	8/51
1955	30	38	6	706	78*	22.06	–	4	26	1093.1	362	2382	133	17.90	9	3	7/95
1956	25	34	5	320	43*	11.03	–	–	8	959.3	364	1906	132	14.43	8	3	10/53
1956–57	14	16	6	79	17	7.90	–	–	3	387.7	122	875	50	17.52	2	–	6/47
1957	28	28	11	210	44	12.35	–	–	9	1016.5	393	1921	126	15.24	5	2	7/16
1958	28	29	6	325	59	14.13	–	1	11	882.5	330	1651	116	14.23	7	2	8/46
1958–59	10	13	3	107	22*	10.70	–	–	1	282.1	63	655	38	17.23	3	1	5/31
1959	24	30	7	301	28	13.08	–	–	15	797.2	246	1920	78	24.61	5	2	7/38
1962	12	11	2	43	13	4.77	–	–	5	379.5	96	962	51	18.86	5	1	7/73
1963	10	12	5	95	24*	13.57	–	–	4	374	128	828	43	19.25	2	1	7/89
1963–64	2	1	1	0	0*	–	–	–	1	72	13	221	5	44.20	–	–	2/50
1964	8	6	1	110	28	22.00	–	–	2	226	55	577	17	33.94	–	–	4/41
1964–65	4	2	0	6	5	3.00	–	–	1	133.4	23	434	14	31.00	1	–	5/54
Total	450	548	108	7304	113	16.60	2	18	269	15982.1	5236	35791	1944	18.41	27	32	10/53
										670	*185*						

English seasons 1946–59 Laker played for Surrey
English seasons 1962–64 Laker played for Essex
1947–48 & 1953–54: MCC in West Indies

1950–51: Commonwealth team in India
1951–52: Auckland (New Zealand)
1956–57: MCC in South Africa

1958–59: MCC in Australia
1963–64, 1964–65: Cavaliers in West Indies
Italic figures refer to eight-ball overs

Test Career – Match by Match

1947–48 v West Indies

	R	Ct	O	M	R	W
Bridgetown, Barbados	2		37	9	103	7
			30	12	95	2
Port-of-Spain, Trinidad	55		36	10	108	2
	24					
Georgetown, British Guiana	10		36	11	94	2
	6		9	1	34	2
Kingston, Jamaica	6	1	36.4	5	103	3
	6*		2	0	11	0

	M	I	NO	R	HS	Avge	100	50	Ct
Total	4	7	1	109	55	18.16	–	1	1

	O	M	R	W	Avge	5 WI	10 WM	BB
Total	186.4	48	548	18	30.44	1	–	7/103

1948 v Australia

	R	Ct	O	M	R	W
Trent Bridge	63		55	14	138	4
	4					
Lord's	28		7	3	17	0
	0		31.2	6	111	2
Leeds	4		30	8	113	3
	15*		32	11	93	0

	M	I	NO	R	HS	Avge	100	50	Ct
Total	3	6	1	114	63	22.80	–	1	–

	O	M	R	W	Avge	5 WI	10 WM	BB
Total	155.2	42	472	9	52.44	–	–	4/138

Test Career – Match by Match–*continued*

1949 v New Zealand

		R	Ct		O	M	R	W
The Oval		0			3	0	11	0
					29	6	78	4

	M	I	NO	R	HS	Avge	100	50	Ct
Total	1	1	0	0	0	–	–	–	–

	O	M	R	W	Avge	5 WI	10 WM	BB
Total	32	6	89	4	22.25	–	–	4/78

1950 v West Indies

	R	Ct	O	M	R	W
Old Trafford	4		17	5	43	0
	40		14	4.	43	1

	M	I	NO	R	HS	Avge	100	50	Ct
Total	1	2	0	44	40	22.00	–	–	–

	O	M	R	W	Avge	5 WI	10 WM	BB
Total	31	9	86	1	–	–	–	1/43

1951 v South Africa

	R	Ct	O	M	R	W
Old Trafford	27		27	7	47	1
			19	3	42	3
The Oval	6	1	37	12	64	4
	13*		28	8	55	6

	M	I	NO	R	HS	Avge	100	50	Ct
Total	2	3	1	46	27	23.00	–	–	1

	O	M	R	W	Avge	5 WI	10 WM	BB
Total	111	30	208	14	14.85	1	1	6/55

Test Career – Match by Match–*continued*

1952 v India

	R	Ct	O	M	R	W
Leeds	15	1	22.3	9	39	4
			13	4	17	0
Lord's	23*	1	12	5	21	0
			39	15	102	4
Old Trafford	0	1	2	0	7	0
The Oval	6*		2	0	3	0

	M	I	NO	R	HS	Avge	100	50	Ct
Total	4	4	2	44	23*	22.00	–	–	3

	O	M	R	W	Avge	5 WI	10 WM	BB
Total	90.3	33	189	8	23.62	–	–	4/39

1953 v Australia

	R	Ct	O	M	R	W
Old Trafford	5		17	3	42	1
			9	5	11	2
Leeds	10		9	1	33	0
	48		2	0	17	1
The Oval	1		5	0	34	1
			16.5	2	75	4

	M	I	NO	R	HS	Avge	100	50	Ct
Total	3	4	0	64	48	16.00	–	–	–

	O	M	R	W	Avge	5 WI	10 WM	BB
Total	58.5	11	212	9	23.55	–	–	4/75

Test Career – Match by Match–*continued*

1953–54 v West Indies

	R	Ct	O	M	R	W
Bridgetown, Barbados	1		30.1	6	81	4
	0		30	13	62	0
Georgetown, British Guiana	27		21	11	32	2
			36	18	56	2
Port-of-Spain, Trinidad	7*	1	50	8	154	2
Kingston, Jamaica	9	1	4	1	13	0
	1		50	27	71	4

	M	I	NO	R	HS	Avge	100	50	Ct
Total	4	5	1	44	27	11.00	–	–	3

	O	M	R	W	Avge	5 WI	10 WM	BB
Total	221.1	84	469	14	33.50	–	–	4/71

1954 v Pakistan

	R	Ct	O	M	R	W
Lord's	13*		22	12	17	1
			10.2	5	22	1

	M	I	NO	R	HS	Avge	100	50	Ct
Total	1	1	1	13	13*	–	–	–	–

	O	M	R	W	Avge	5 WI	10 WM	BB
Total	32.2	17	39	2	19.50	–	–	1/17

1955 v South Africa

	R	Ct	O	M	R	W
The Oval	2		23	13	28	2
	12		37.4	18	56	5

	M	I	NO	R	HS	Avge	100	50	Ct
Total	1	2	0	14	12	7.00	–	–	–

	O	M	R	W	Avge	5 WI	10 WM	BB
Total	60.4	31	84	7	12.00	1	–	5/56

Test Career – Match by Match–*continued*

1956 v Australia

	R	Ct	O	M	R	W
Trent Bridge	9*		29.1	11	58	4
			30	19	29	2
Lord's	12		29.1	10	47	3
	4		7	3	17	0
Leeds	5		29	10	58	5
			41.3	21	55	6
Old Trafford	3		16.4	4	37	9
			51.2	23	53	10
The Oval	4		32	12	80	4
			18	14	8	3

	M	I	NO	R	HS	Avge	100	50	Ct
Total	5	6	1	37	12	7.40	–	–	–

	O	M	R	W	Avge	5 WI	10 WM	BB
Total	283.5	127	442	46	9.60	4	2	10/53

1956–57 v South Africa

	R	Ct	O	M	R	W
Johannesburg	0		21	10	33	1
	3*		2	1	5	1
Cape Town	0		28	8	65	1
			14.1	9	7	2
Durban	0*		12	1	47	0
	6	1	18	7	29	2
Johannesburg	17		15	3	49	1
	5		7	1	26	1
Port Elizabeth	6		14	1	37	1
	3*		14	5	26	1

	M	I	NO	R	HS	Avge	100	50	Ct
Total	5	9	3	40	17	6.66	–	–	1

	O	M	R	W	Avge	5 WI	10 WM	BB
Total	145.1	46	324	11	29.45	–	–	2/7

Test Career – Match by Match–*continued*

1957 v West Indies

	R	Ct	O	M	R	W
Edgbaston	7		54	17	119	4
			24	20	13	2
Trent Bridge	–	1	62	27	101	3
			43	14	98	1
Leeds	1		17	4	24	2
			6.2	1	16	1
The Oval	10*		23	12	39	3
			17	4	38	2

	M	I	NO	R	HS	Avge	100	50	Ct
Total	4	3	1	18	10*	9.00	–	–	1

	O	M	R	W	Avge	5 WI	10 WM	BB
Total	246.2	99	448	18	24.88	–	–	4/119

1958 v New Zealand

	R	Ct	O	M	R	W
Edgbaston	11*	1	5	2	9	1
			9	4	14	1
Lord's	1	1	12	6	13	4
			13	8	24	1
Leeds	–		22	11	17	5
			36	23	27	3
The Oval	15		14	3	44	1
			20	10	25	1

	M	I	NO	R	HS	Avge	100	50	Ct
Total	4	3	1	27	15	13.50	–	–	2

	O	M	R	W	Avge	5 WI	10 WM	BB
Total	131	67	173	17	10.17	1	–	5/17

Test Career – Match by Match–*continued*

1958–59 v Australia

			R	Ct	O	M	R	W
Brisbane			13		10.1	3	15	2
			15		17	3	39	1
Melbourne			22*		12	1	47	0
			3		4	1	7	1
Sydney			2		46	9	107	5
					8	3	10	2

	M	I	NO	R	HS	Avge	100	50	Ct
Total	4	7	2	62	22*	12.40	–	–	–

	O	M	R	W	Avge	5 WI	10 WM	BB
Total	127.6	24	318	15	21.20	1	–	5/107

Test figures against each country

	M	I	NO	R	HS	Avge	100	50	Ct	O	M	R	W	Avge	5 WI	10 WM	BB
Australia	15	23	4	277	63	14.57	–	1	–	498	180	1444	79	18.27	5	2	10/53
										127.6	*24*						
India	4	4	2	44	23*	22.00	–	–	3	90.3	33	189	8	23.62	–	–	4/39
New Zealand	5	4	1	27	15	9.00	–	–	2	163	73	262	21	12.47	1	–	5/17
Pakistan	1	1	1	13	13*	–	–	–	–	32.2	17	39	2	19.50	–	–	1/17
South Africa	8	14	4	100	27	10.00	–	–	2	171.4	61	616	32	19.25	2	1	6/55
										145.1	*46*						
West Indies	13	17	3	215	55	15.35	–	1	5	685.1	240	1551	51	30.41	1	–	7/103
Total	46	63	15	676	63	14.08	–	2	12	1640.4	604	4101	193	21.24	9	3	10/53
										272.7	*70*						

Italic figures refer to eight-ball overs

174

Test cricket – Record at each ground

	M	I	NO	R	HS	Avge	100	50	Ct	O	M	R	W	Avge	5 WI	10 WM	BB
England																	
Leeds	6	7	1	98	48	16.33	–	–	1	260.2	103	509	30	16.96	5	2	6/55
Lord's	5	7	2	81	28	16.20	–	–	2	182.5	73	391	16	24.43	–	–	4/13
Old Trafford	5	6	0	79	40	13.16	–	–	1	173	54	325	27	12.03	2	1	10/53
Oval	8	10	3	69	15	9.85	–	–	1	305.3	114	638	40	15.95	2	1	6/55
Trent Bridge	3	3	1	76	63	38.00	–	1	1	219.1	85	424	14	30.28	–	–	4/58
Edgbaston	2	2	1	18	11*	–	–	–	1	92	43	155	8	19.37	–	–	4/119
Total	29	35	8	421	63	15.59	–	1	7	1232.5	472	2442	135	18.08	9	4	10/64
Australia																	
Brisbane	1	2	0	28	15	14.00	–	–	–	27.1	6	54	3	18.00	–	–	2/15
Melbourne	2	4	2	32	22*	16.00	–	–	–	46.5	6	147	5	29.40	–	–	4/93
Sydney	1	1	0	2	2	–	–	–	–	54	12	117	7	16.71	1	–	5/107
Total	4	7	2	62	22*	12.40	–	–	–	127.6	24	318	15	21.20	1	–	5/107
South Africa																	
Johannesburg	2	4	1	25	17	8.33	–	–	–	45	15	113	4	28.25	–	–	1/5
Cape Town	1	1	0	0	0	–	–	–	–	42.1	17	72	3	24.00	–	–	2/7
Durban	1	2	1	6	6	–	–	–	1	30	8	76	2	38.00	–	–	2/29
Port Elizabeth	1	2	1	9	6	–	–	–	–	28	6	63	2	31.50	–	–	1/26
Total	5	9	3	40	17	6.66	–	–	1	145.1	46	324	11	29.45	–	–	2/7
West Indies																	
Bridgetown	2	3	0	3	3	1.00	–	–	–	127.1	40	341	13	26.23	1	–	7/103
Georgetown	2	3	0	43	27	14.33	–	–	–	102	41	216	8	27.00	–	–	2/32
Kingston	2	3	1	21	9	10.50	–	–	3	92.4	33	198	7	28.28	–	–	4/31
Port-of-Spain	2	3	1	86	55	43.00	–	1	1	86	18	262	4	65.50	–	–	2/108
Total	8	12	2	153	55	15.30	–	1	4	407.5	132	1017	32	31.78	1	–	7/103

Test Dismissals

99 Caught; 52 bowled; 32 lbw; 10 stumped.

Batsmen dismissed by Laker in Test Matches

11 C. L. Walcott (W Indies)
10 K. R. Miller (Aust)
 7 I. W. Johnson, J. W. Burke, K. D. Mackay (all Aust)
 6 R. Benaud, C. C. McDonald (both Aust)
 5 R. A. McLean (S Africa)
 4 R. G. Archer, A. K. Davidson, R. N. Harvey, R. R. Lindwall (all Aust); W. R. Endean, C. B. van Ryneveld (both S Africa)
 3 I. D. Craig, A. T. W. Grout, A. R. Morris (all Aust); R. J. Christiani, W. Ferguson, J. D. C. Goddard, G. E. Gomez, S. Ramadhin, O. G. Smith (all W Indies); A. R. MacGibbon (N Zealand)
 2 P. J. P. Burge, L. V. Maddocks (both Aust), J. E. Cheetham, P. N. F. Mansell, A. J. Pithey, E. A. B. Rowan, J. H. B. Waite (all S Africa); D. st. E. Atkinson, F. C. M. Alexander, G. M. Carew, C. A. McWatt, J. B. Stollmeyer, E. D. Weekes, E. A. V. Williams (all W Indies); J. C. Alabaster, H. B. Cave, N. S. Harford, L. S. M. Miller, W. R. Playle, J. R. Reid (all New Zealand); D. G. Phadkar (India)
 1 S. G. Barnes, A. L. Hassett, G. B. Hole, G. R. Langley, N. C. O'Neill, R. A. Saggers (all Aust); N. A. T. Adcock, C. A. R. Duckworth, G. M. Fullerton, P. S. Heine, H. J. Keith, D. J. McGlew, M. G. Melle, A. D. Nourse, J. C. Watkins (all S Africa); B. M. Gaskin, R. Gilchrist, G. A. Headley, R. Kanhai, F. M. King, B. H. Pairaudeau, K. R. Richards, G. S. Sobers (all W Indies); T. B. Burtt, J. Cowie, J. W. Darcy, T. Meale, E. C. Petrie, G. O. Rabone, B. Sutcliffe (all N Zealand), Ghulam Ahmed, V. L. Manjrekhar, M. H. Mankad, M. K. Mantri, G. S. Ramchand, S. G. Shinde (all India); Hanif Mohammed, Imtiaz Ahmed (both Pakistan)

Of those dismissed by Laker, 47 could be claimed to be specialist batsmen, 18 middle-order batsmen, 18 tail-enders.

Record for Surrey against each team

	M	I	NO	R	HS	Avge	100	50	Ct	O	M	R	W	Avge	5 WI	10 WM	BB
Derbys	12	15	1	142	38	10.14	–	–	12	392.4	124	821	53	15.49	2	–	5/57
Essex	21	31	8	344	56*	14.95	–	1	13	826.4	222	1862	106	17.56	8	3	7/84
Glamorgan	19	25	3	404	61	18.36	–	2	15	734.3	254	1399	79	17.70	5	1	6/67
Gloucs	17	25	3	414	113	18.81	1	–	11	715.4	278	1270	110	11.54	8	3	8/45
Hants	17	20	6	301	81	21.50	–	2	8	667.2	189	1592	85	18.72	6	–	8/69
Kent	18	23	5	409	99	22.72	–	1	13	766	265	1484	95	15.62	8	1	7/47
Lancs	11	14	2	196	55	16.33	–	1	8	367	135	642	37	17.35	1	1	6/41
Leics	18	16	2	319	59	22.78	–	2	15	801.3	310	1356	72	18.83	4	–	6/25
Middlesex	21	30	4	435	60	16.73	–	1	12	775.3	219	1937	105	18.44	9	2	8/57
Northants	16	23	5	483	89	26.83	–	2	11	611.3	191	1398	67	20.86	6	1	7/57
Notts	23	21	4	296	42*	17.41	–	–	16	809.11	297	1718	87	19.74	5	–	7/16
Somerset	14	13	3	160	39	16.00	–	–	18	477.2	172	962	64	15.03	6	1	7/59
Sussex	11	14	5	248	78*	27.55	–	2	6	440	143	940	60	15.66	2	2	8/46
Warwicks	11	15	2	162	35	12.46	–	–	10	360.4	92	907	53	17.11	4	1	8/42
Worcs	14	15	4	97	20*	8.81	–	–	14	517	181	1049	75	13.98	5	2	7/61
Yorkshire	17	26	2	309	66	12.87	1	1	7	626.4	229	1241	57	21.77	3	1	6/23
Cambridge	13	9	2	285	100	40.71	–	–	12	494.2	181	907	39	23.25	1	–	5/54
Oxford	2	3	0	19	17	6.33	–	–	1	62.1	18	127	11	11.54	1	–	5/24
MCC	11	16	6	149	43*	14.90	–	–	8	337	84	750	61	12.29	5	3	8/51
Australia	5	7	1	98	43	16.33	–	–	4	172	45	443	19	23.31	1	1	10/88
S Africa	1	2	0	7	7	3.50	–	–	1	46	12	127	6	21.16	1	–	5/56
W Indies	4	6	0	127	30	21.16	–	–	2	147	46	301	9	33.44	–	–	4/48
N Zealand	4	5	1	51	15*	12.75	–	–	2	148	47	317	13	24.38	1	–	6/112
India	3	5	0	28	16	5.60	–	–	2	118	29	274	15	18.26	1	1	6/64
Pakistan	1	1	0	4	4	–	–	–	1	43	17	63	3	21.00	–	–	3/63
Services	2	2	0	3	3	1.50	–	–	1	42	9	121	6	20.16	–	–	3/43
The Rest	3	5	1	41	17*	10.25	–	–	–	92	23	228	8	28.50	–	–	3/32
Total	309	387	70	5531	113	17.44	2	15	223	11590.4	3812	24236	1395	17.37	93	24	10/88

Record for Surrey – home and away

Home matches

	M	I	NO	R	HS	Avge	100	50	Ct	O	M	R	W	Avge	5 WI	10 WM	BB
The Oval	151	186	24	2472	113	15.25	1	5	128	5482.5	1818	11291	647	17.45	42	11	10/88
Guildford	13	11	2	282	100	31.33	1	1	8	472.2	148	916	54	16.96	4	1	7/38
Kingston	2	2	1	0	0*	–	–	–	–	18	3	48	2	24.00	–	–	1/22
Total	166	199	27	2754	113	16.01	2	6	136	5973.1	1969	12255	703	17.43	46	12	10/88
Away matches	143	188	43	2777	66	19.15	–	9	87	5617.3	1843	11981	692	17.31	47	12	8/45
Total	309	387	70	5531	113	17.44	2	15	223	11590.4	3812	24236	1395	17.37	93	24	10/88

Away matches – ground by ground

	M	I	NO	R	HS	Avge	100	50	Ct	O	M	R	W	Avge	5 WI	10 WM	BB
Bath	1	1	1	6	6*	–	–	–	2	61.5	23	122	9	13.35	1	–	7/59
Blackheath	8	11	4	155	40	22.14	–	–	3	352.4	132	645	37	17.43	2	–	6/60
Bournemouth	3	4	1	69	43	23.00	–	–	2	132	42	306	10	30.60	–	–	3/57
Bradford	3	3	0	32	14	10.66	–	–	2	150.1	69	258	14	18.42	1	–	6/23
Brentwood	1	1	0	2	2	–	–	–	1	28	6	60	0	–	–	–	
Bristol	2	2	0	74	39	37.00	–	–	1	124	58	150	16	9.37	1	1	8/45
Cambridge	6	4	1	100	44	33.33	–	–	5	234.4	104	378	20	18.90	–	–	4/38
Cardiff	5	8	0	110	61	13.75	–	1	4	222.2	74	441	23	19.17	1	–	5/86
Chelmsford	2	3	0	54	33	18.00	–	–	1	109.2	32	227	18	12.61	2	1	7/94
Cheltenham	3	5	1	96	32*	24.00	–	–	3	93.2	39	166	15	11.06	1	–	5/30
Chesterfield	3	3	0	10	4	3.33	–	–	2	118.1	32	257	18	14.27	1	–	5/64
Clacton	1	2	2	17	13*	–	–	–	1	34	9	92	4	23.00	–	–	3/38
Colchester	1	1	0	19	19	–	–	–	1	31	8	91	2	45.50	–	–	2/50
Coventry	1	2	0	32	12	16.00	–	–	1	51	6	185	10	18.50	1	1	7/95
Derby	2	3	0	21	12	7.00	–	–	3	61.3	16	140	9	15.55	–	–	4/64
Dudley	1	1	0	8	8	–	–	–	2	59.3	15	144	8	18.00	1	–	6/66
Edgbaston	2	1	0	0	0	–	–	–	–	86.5	20	271	7	38.71	–	–	3/94
Gloucester	3	6	1	28	16	5.60	–	–	–	122	39	275	25	11.00	2	1	6/27
Hastings	1	2	1	23	18	–	–	–	–	56	15	121	5	24.20	–	–	4/49
Hove	4	6	2	98	53*	24.50	–	1	2	143.5	45	369	28	13.17	1	1	8/46
Ilford	3	6	3	101	56*	33.66	–	1	1	159.2	52	416	18	23.11	1	–	7/84
Kettering	1	2	1	51	33*	–	–	–	1	38.5	15	94	11	8.54	2	1	6/58
Kidderminster	1	1	0	7	7	–	–	–	–	42.2	14	86	4	21.50	–	–	3/30
Leeds	2	4	0	98	66	24.50	–	1	–	49	15	107	2	53.50	–	–	1/17
Leicester	8	8	0	125	53	15.62	–	1	6	347.1	134	592	33	17.93	2	–	6/55
Leyton	1	2	0	16	12	8.00	–	–	–	8	2	13	2	6.50	–	–	2/13
Llanelli	1	1	0	20	20	–	–	–	–	44	17	67	6	11.16	1	–	6/67

Away matches – ground by ground–*continued*

Lord's	21	31	8	365	60	15.86	–	1	11	700.4	184	1696	114	14.87	11	4	8/51
Loughborough	1	1	0	42	42	–	–	–	1	42	18	43	1	–	–	–	1/19
Northampton	4	7	1	161	43*	26.83	–	–	2	145.3	43	348	11	31.63	–	–	3/86
Old Trafford	5	7	0	109	55	15.57	–	1	2	152.1	46	318	14	22.71	–	–	4/37
Peterborough	2	1	0	25	25	–	–	–	2	46.4	9	124	7	17.71	1	–	6/55
Pontypridd	1	1	0	13	13	–	–	–	2	24.2	11	34	3	11.33	–	–	3/19
Portsmouth	4	6	3	56	19	18.66	–	–	2	158.4	37	465	20	23.25	1	–	8/69
Romford	1	2	1	15	14	–	–	–	–	9	2	30	2	15.00	–	–	2/30
Rushden	1	2	0	27	17	13.50	–	–	1	49.2	16	99	9	11.00	1	–	7/57
Scarborough	1	1	1	17	17*	–	–	–	–	30	8	68	4	17.00	–	–	3/32
Sheffield	3	5	1	42	16	10.50	–	–	1	85	30	178	6	29.66	1	–	4/56
Southend	2	2	0	37	34	18.50	–	–	2	86	30	163	10	16.30	–	–	5/32
Southampton	2	2	1	54	51	–	–	1	–	125.3	40	258	16	16.12	2	–	6/53
Swansea	3	4	2	135	53	67.50	–	1	1	157	50	324	19	17.05	2	1	5/53
Taunton	3	2	0	31	19	15.50	–	–	3	69	24	137	11	12.45	1	–	5/22
Trent Bridge	11	10	3	169	42*	24.14	–	–	5	437.5	155	950	45	21.11	3	–	7/16
Wells	1	1	0	26	26	–	–	–	1	45.5	16	70	7	10.00	–	–	4/24
Weston	2	3	2	43	39	–	–	–	1	78.4	25	186	10	18.60	1	–	6/66
Worcester	5	7	2	38	11*	7.60	–	–	6	213.3	76	417	29	14.37	2	1	7/61
Total	143	188	43	2777	66	19.15	–	9	87	5617.3	1843	11981	692	17.31	47	12	8/45

Record for Essex against each team

	M	I	NO	R	HS	Avge	100	50	Ct	O	M	R	W	Avge	5 WI	10 WM	BB
Derbys	1	2	0	15	12	7.50	–	–	1	26	9	74	2	37.00	–	–	2/74
Glamorgan	2	4	2	67	27	33.50	–	–	–	57	15	150	5	30.00	–	–	3/78
Gloucs	2	1	0	2	2	–	–	–	1	46	15	112	2	56.00	–	–	1/30
Hants	1	–		–	–	–	–	–	–	32	9	70	3	23.33	–	–	2/33
Kent	2	1	0	28	28	–	–	–	1	91.4	17	260	17	15.29	2	1	7/73
Lancashire	4	2	0	22	22	11.00	–	–	2	145	39	341	13	26.23	–	–	4/81
Leics	3	4	1	18	9	6.00	–	–	2	94.1	28	209	18	11.61	1	–	7/89
Middlesex	2	1	0	20	20	–	–	–	1	65	13	133	2	66.50	–	–	1/40
Northants	2	2	1	27	16	–	–	–	2	87	36	162	12	13.50	1	1	6/49
Notts	2	2	2	3	2*	–	–	–	–	45	18	97	3	32.33	–	–	2/66
Somerset	1	2	0	17	13	8.50	–	–	–	49.1	14	130	5	26.00	–	–	5/46
Sussex	1	–		–	–	–	–	–	–	52.5	12	128	7	18.28	1	–	6/49
Warwicks	3	3	1	18	17*	9.00	–	–	–	69	19	183	7	26.14	1	–	6/52
Worcs	3	4	1	10	4	3.33	–	–	1	87	32	221	8	27.62	–	–	4/32
Yorkshire	1	1	0	1	1	–	–	–	–	33	3	97	7	13.85	–	–	4/42
Total	30	29	8	248	28	11.80	–	–	11	979.5	279	2367	111	21.32	7	2	7/73

Record for Essex – home and away

Home matches

	M	I	NO	R	HS	Avge	100	50	Ct	O	M	R	W	Avge	5 WI	10 WM	BB
Brentwood	4	3	0	39	22	13.00	–	–	–	160.1	40	382	13	29.38	1	1	5/46
Clacton	1	1	0	1	1	–	–	–	–	33	3	97	7	13.85	–	–	4/42
Colchester	1	1	0	1	1	–	–	–	–	13	0	52	6	8.66	1	–	6/52
Ilford	4	4	0	52	28	13.00	–	–	2	119	31	300	10	30.00	–	–	4/41
Leyton	1	1	0	0	0	–	–	–	1	13	3	33	1	–	–	–	1/33
Romford	2	2	1	7	4	–	–	–	2	89	37	173	10	17.30	1	1	6/49
Total	13	12	1	100	28	9.09	–	–	5	427.1	114	1037	47	22.06	3	1	6/49

Away matches

	M	I	NO	R	HS	Avge	100	50	Ct	O	M	R	W	Avge	5 WI	10 WM	BB
Bristol	2	1	0	2	2	–	–	–	1	46	15	12	2	56.00	–	–	1/30
Dover	1	–	–	–	–	–	–	–	1	57.4	12	159	13	12.23	2	1	7/73
Edgbaston	1	2	1	17	17*	–	–	–	–	32	14	65	1	–	–	–	1/62
Hinckley	1	1	0	0	0	–	–	–	–	28.1	9	61	7	8.71	–	–	4/22
Leicester	1	2	1	9	9	–	–	–	1	31	7	89	7	12.71	1	–	7/89
Liverpool	1	–	–	–	–	–	–	–	1	55	15	128	5	25.60	–	–	4/81
Lord's	1	1	0	20	20	–	–	–	1	31	8	61	1	–	–	–	1/40
Northampton	1	2	1	27	16	–	–	–	1	19	3	56	2	28.00	–	–	2/56
Southampton	1	–	–	–	–	–	–	–	–	32	9	70	3	23.33	–	–	2/33
Swansea	2	4	2	67	27	33.50	–	–	–	57	15	150	5	30.00	–	–	3/78
Trent Bridge	2	2	2	3	2*	–	–	–	–	45	18	97	3	32.33	–	–	2/66
Worcester	2	2	0	3	2	1.50	–	–	–	66	28	154	8	19.25	–	–	4/32
Worthing	1	–	–	–	–	–	–	–	–	52.5	12	128	7	18.28	1	–	6/49
Total	17	17	7	148	27	14.80	–	–	6	552.4	165	1330	64	20.78	4	1	7/73
Grand Total	30	29	8	248	28	11.80	–	–	11	979.5	279	2367	111	21.32	7	2	7/73

Record for other teams in England

	M	I	NO	R	HS	Avge	100	50	Ct	O	M	R	W	Avge	5 WI	10 WM	BB
MCC v Essex	1	1	1	1	1*	–	–	–	1	43	21	51	7	7.28	1	–	7/36
v Yorks	2	2	0	21	17	10.50	–	–	1	74.4	21	174	12	14.50	–	–	3/27
v Australia	1	2	1	20	16*	–	–	–	–	37	10	127	3	42.33	–	–	3/127
v India	1	1	0	16	16	–	–	–	–	43	10	97	1	–	–	–	1/56
v N Zealand	1	1	1	10	10*	–	–	–	–	38	14	57	1	–	–	–	1/57
Total for MCC	6	7	3	68	17	17.00	–	–	2	235.4	76	506	24	21.08	1	–	7/36
P.F. Warner's XI	1	2	0	12	10	6.00	–	–	–	66.2	18	182	8	22.75	1	1	6/109
England XI																	
v Comm'lth	3	6	2	45	18	11.25	–	–	2	80.4	12	307	9	34.11	–	–	3/43
v India	1	–	–	–	–	–	–	–	–	10	3	23	0	–	–	–	–
v Pakistan	1	2	0	25	13	12.50	–	–	–	18	3	60	0	–	–	–	–
v The Rest	2	1	1	6	6*	–	–	–	–	49	20	83	11	7.54	1	1	8/2
Players v Gents	3	4	0	25	8	6.25	–	–	1	107.1	35	242	14	17.28	1	–	6/48
Leveson-Gower's XI																	
v Australia	1	1	0	7	7	–	–	–	–	20	4	95	1	–	–	–	1/95
v MCC XI	1	1	0	10	10	–	–	–	1	39.1	4	169	6	28.16	1	–	5/97
South v Glam	1	2	0	60	33	30.00	–	–	.	34	5	89	0	–	–	–	–
v Rest	2	2	1	46	26	–	–	–	–	16	1	49	4	12.25	–	–	2/5
Surrey XI v Rest	1	2	1	25	17*	–	–	–	–	31	7	69	1	–	–	–	1/42
Total	23	30	8	329	33	14.95	–	–	6	707	188	1874	78	24.02	5	1	8/2

Ground records for 'other' matches

	M	I	NO	R	HS	Avge	100	50	Ct	O	M	R	W	Avge	5 WI	10 WM	BB
Bradford	1	1	1	6	6*	–	–	–	–	32	16	46	10	4.60	1	1	8/2
Edgbaston	1	–	–	–	–	–	–	–	–	17	4	37	1	–	–	–	1/25
Hastings	7	10	3	108	26	15.42	–	–	2	156.2	28	516	15	34.40	1	–	6/109
Kingston	2	4	1	45	17*	15.00	–	–	–	65.4	16	174	7	24.85	–	–	3/43
Lord's	9	11	3	93	17	11.62	–	–	3	342.5	111	748	38	19.68	2	–	7/36
Scarborough	2	2	0	17	10	8.50	–	–	1	59.1	8	264	7	37.71	1	–	5/97
Swansea	1	2	0	60	33	30.00	–	–	–	34	5	89	0	–	–	–	–
Total	23	30	8	329	33	14.95	–	–	6	707	188	1874	78	24.02	5	1	8/2

Career analysis – country by country

	M	I	NO	R	HS	Avge	100	50	Ct	O	M	R	W	Avge	5 WI	10 WM
England	391	481	94	6529	113	16.87	2	16	247	14510.2	4751	30919	1719	17.98	112	30
Aust.	10	13	3	107	22*	10.70	–	–	1	282.1	63	655	38	17.23	3	1
India	10	10	1	171	61	19.00	–	1	5	315.2	131	579	36	16.08	3	–
N Zealand	4	4	0	77	35	19.25	–	–	3	228.1	88	379	24	15.79	3	1
S Africa	14	16	6	79	17	7.90	–	–	3	387.1	122	875	50	17.50	2	–
W Indies	21	24	4	341	55	17.05	–	1	10	928.2	266	2384	77	30.96	4	–
Total	450	548	108	7304	113	16.60	2	18	269	15982.1	5236	35791	1944	18.41	127	32
										670	185					

INDEX